OF THE
GOSPEL

RESOURCES FOR THE
CHRISTIAN
YEAR
FOR THE USE
OF UNITED METHODISTS

Abingdon Press/Nashville
1979

SEASONS OF THE GOSPEL

ISBN 0-687-37130-9

MANUFACTURED BY THE PARTHENON PRESS AT
NASHVILLE, TENNESSEE, UNITED STATES OF AMERICA

CONTENTS

PREFACE

This volume of resources for the Christian Year is the sixth in the Supplemental Worship Resources series—originally called the Alternate Rituals series—developed and sponsored by the Section on Worship of the Board of Discipleship of The United Methodist Church.

When The United Methodist Church was formed in 1968, *The Book of Discipline* provided (Par. 1388) that:

> The hymnals of The United Methodist Church are the hymnals of The Evangelical United Brethren Church and *The Methodist Hymnal* [later retitled The *Book of Hymns*]; the Ritual of the Church is that contained in the *Book of Ritual* of The Evangelical United Brethren Church, 1959, and *The Book of Worship for Church and Home* of The Methodist Church.

It quickly became apparent, however, that there was a need for supplemental worship resources which, while not taking the place of these official resources, would provide alternatives that more fully reflect developments in the contemporary ecumenical church. The General Conference of 1970 authorized the Commission on Worship to begin work in this area, and the General Conferences of 1972 and 1976 authorized the Board of Discipleship "to develop standards and resources for the conduct of public worship in the churches" (1976 *Book of Discipline*, Par. 1316.2). The resulting series of publications began with

The Sacrament of the Lord's Supper: An Alternate Text 1972 (Supplemental Worship Resources 1), which was published both in a text edition and later (1975) in a music edition. Intensive work during the next four years led to the publication in 1976 of *A Service of Baptism, Confirmation, and Renewal: An Alternate Text 1976* (SWR 2), *Word and Table: A Basic Pattern of Sunday Worship for United Methodists* (SWR 3), and *Ritual in a New Day: An Invitation* (SWR 4). IN 1973 the process was begun toward the publication of *A Service of Christian Marriage* (SWR 5) and *A Service of Death and Resurrection* (SWR 7).

The present and sixth publication in this series is an especially close companion and sequel to *Word and Table*. Both deal with a basic pattern of Sunday worship for United Methodists. Chapter 5 of *Word and Table*, "The Christian Year: An Alternative Calendar and Lectionary," laid the foundations upon which *Seasons of the Gospel* builds and should be studied for the fuller understanding of the present volume. In particular, the reader of *Seasons of the Gospel* can profitably read the sections on "Uses of the Lectionary" and "The Ecumenical Calendar and Lectionary: A History" on pages 58-68 of *Word and Table* as well as the "Special Days" lectionary on page 57.

Further publications dealing with this basic pattern of Sunday worship for United Methodists are to be published soon. *From Ashes to Fire* will deal in more detailed way with the seasons of Lent and Easter through the Day of Pentecost. *At the Lord's Table* will supply further texts and suggestions for the Lord's Supper to supplement the single text published in 1972.

Seasons of the Gospel, like the other publications in this series, represents the corporate work of the writers and consultants, and of the Section on Worship acting as an editorial committee. This committee determined the original specifications and carefully examined and edited the manuscript before approving it for publication. Professor James F. White of Perkins School of Theology at Southern Methodist University was the writer of chapter 2 and was the principal writer of the manuscript. Four times during the writing of the manuscript he held consultations with Professor Don E. Saliers of Candler School of Theology at Emory University and Dr. Hoyt L. Hickman of the Section on Worship staff, both members of the task force that wrote *Word and Table*. Dr. Hickman drafted the table of Psalms and revised lectionary in chapter 3 and compiled the indexes to the Scripture lections and Psalms in chapter 5. The Rev. H. Myron Braun, Editor of *Music Ministry* magazine, drafted the lists of suggested hymns for chapter 3 as a compilation and revision of similar lists published in *Music Ministry* beginning with the December 1975 issue. He also compiled the Index to the Hymns in chapter 5. Sister Kathy Hughes, R.S.C.J., assisted in revising the opening prayers. Collation of materials used in chapter 3 and general manuscript preparation were done by Hoyt L. Hickman. Everland Robinson, and Davelyn Vignaud in the office of the Section on Worship.

The members and staff of the Section on Worship, listed below, wish to thank the persons named above and many others who have shared with us ideas and resources for the Christian year. Reactions to this volume, comments or suggestions, and any materials that have been created or discovered are welcomed by the Section on Worship, PO Box 840, Nashville, Tennessee 37202. We commend this volume to the use of local churches in the hope that it will be useful in the worship of God and the proclamation of the gospel of Jesus Christ.

Bishop Robert E. Goodrich, Jr., Chairperson, Section on
    Worship
James F. White, Chairperson,
    Editorial Committee and Principal Writer
Paul F. Abel
Phyllis Close
Edward L. Duncan
Judy Gilreath
Kay Hereford
Judith Kelsey-Powell
Marilynn Mabee

L. Doyle Masters
William B. McClain
Louise H. Shown
Carlton R. Young
Philip E. Baker, Ex Officio,
   representing the Fellowship of United Methodist
   Musicians
Elise M. Shoemaker, Ex Officio,
   representing the United Methodist Society for Wor-
   ship
Roberto Escamilla,
Associate General Secretary
Hoyt L. Hickman, Assistant General Secretary
Thom C. Jones, Staff

—I—

THE CALENDAR

ADVENT
  First Sunday in Advent
  Second Sunday in Advent
  Third Sunday in Advent
  Fourth Sunday in Advent
CHRISTMAS SEASON
  Christmas or the Nativity of Jesus Christ
    (Christmas Eve and Christmas Day)
  First Sunday after Christmas
    *May be celebrated on December 25 when it falls on a
    Sunday and the Christmas lections have been used on
    Christmas Eve.*
  [Second Sunday after Christmas]
  The Epiphany or the Manifestation of God in Jesus
    Christ (January 6)
    May be celebrated the first Sunday in January.
SEASON AFTER THE EPIPHANY
  First Sunday after the Epiphany or the Baptism of the
    Lord
    (Sunday after January 6)
    *If Sunday falls on January 7, it is suggested that the
    Epiphany and the Baptism of the Lord be celebrated
    together.*
  Second Sunday after the Epiphany
  Third Sunday after the Epiphany

9

[Fourth Sunday after the Epiphany]
[Fifth Sunday after the Epiphany]
[Sixth Sunday after the Epiphany]
[Seventh Sunday after the Epiphany]
[Eighth Sunday after the Epiphany]
Last Sunday after the Epiphany or the Transfiguration of the Lord
Regardless of the number of Sundays after the Epiphany

LENT
Ash Wednesday *(seventh Wednesday before Easter)*
First Sunday in Lent
Second Sunday in Lent
Third Sunday in Lent
Fourth Sunday in Lent
Fifth Sunday in Lent
Palm/Passion Sunday
Monday in Holy Week
Tuesday in Holy Week
Wednesday in Holy Week
Maundy Thursday
Good Friday

EASTER SEASON
Easter Eve or Easter Vigil or the First Service of Easter
Easter Day or the Resurrection of the Lord or the Second Service of Easter
Second Sunday of Easter
Third Sunday of Easter
Fourth Sunday of Easter
Fifth Sunday of Easter
Sixth Sunday of Easter
Ascension Day *(fortieth day—sixth Thursday—of Easter)*
May be celebrated on the Seventh Sunday of Easter.
Seventh Sunday of Easter
Day of Pentecost or the Descent of the Holy Spirit

SEASON AFTER PENTECOST
First Sunday after Pentecost or Trinity Sunday

Second Sunday after Pentecost . . .
Last Sunday after Pentecost or Christ the King
  Regardless of the number of Sundays after Pentecost
All Saints' Day (November 1)
  May be celebrated the first Sunday in November.

—II—
KEEPING TIME WITH THE GOSPEL

Christianity is a religion that takes time seriously. History is where God is made known. Without time, there is no knowledge of God. For it is through actual events happening in historical time that God is revealed. God chooses to make the divine nature and will known by events that take place within the same calendar that measures the daily lives of men and women. God's self-disclosures take place within the same course of time as political events: "In the days of Herod king of Judaea" (Luke 1:5) or "it took place when Quirinius was governor of Syria" (Luke 2:2). God's time is our time, too, measured by a spatial device called a calendar.

When we encounter one of the Eastern religions in which time is insignificant, we realize just how crucial time is to Christian faith. Much non-Western music also suggests a casual indifference to time while typically Western music usually seems to be possessed by a fierce urgency to get somewhere. Our music sweeps on toward climaxes and a finale. Christianity talks, not of salvation in general, but of a salvation accomplished by specific actions of God at specific times and places. It speaks of climactic events and a finale. For Christianity, the ultimate meanings of life are not revealed by universal and timeless aphorisms but by specific acts of God. In the fullness of time, God invades our history, assumes our flesh, heals, teaches, and eats with sinners. There is a specific historical and spatial setting to it all: "It was winter, and the festival of the Dedication was being held in Jerusalem. Jesus was walking in the temple precincts, in Solomon's Portico" (John 10:22-23). And when his work is done, Christ is put to death on a specific day related to the Passover festival of that year, and rises on the third day. It is the same time we inhabit, the time in which we buy groceries, wash the car, and earn a living.

Christian worship is built upon this understanding of time as where God acts in self-revelation. It should not surprise us that Christian worship is structured on a recurring rhythm of the week, the day, and the year—just as is the rest of life. Far from trying to escape time, Christian worship uses time for its basic structure. Present time is used to place us in contact with God's acts in time past. Salvation, as we experience it in worship, is never an abstraction but a reality based on temporal events. Our use of time enables us to commemorate and re-experience those very acts on which salvation is grounded. Christian worship is built on the foundation of time.

History of How We Keep Time

The way we use our time is one of the best indications of what is really important to us. We can always be counted on to find time for those things that we consider most important, though we may not always be willing to admit to others, even to ourselves, what our priorities are. Whether it be making money, political action, or family activities, we find time for putting first those things that matter most for us. Time talks. When we give it to others, we are really giving ourselves. Not only does our use of time show what is important to us but it also indicates who is most significant to our lives. Time, then, is a dead give-away of our priorities. It reveals what we value most by how we allocate this limited resource.

The same thing is true of the church. The church shows what is most important to its life by the way it keeps time. Here again the use of time reveals priorities of faith and practice. One answer to "What do Christians profess?"

13

could be "look how they keep time!" It will give us a good background to look at just how Christians have kept time beginning with the New Testament church.

The faith of the early church is disclosed by the way early Christians organized time. This was not by a systematic or even a planned method but the church's spontaneous response to "the events that have happened among us" (Luke 1:1). The same type of response, the keeping memories alive, also prompted the writing of the gospels that others might be able to follow "the traditions handed down to us by the original eyewitnesses and servants of the Gospel" (Luke 1:2). The use of time was not as systematic as the Evangelists' efforts "to write a connected narrative" (Luke 1:3), but the practice occurred even earlier and has had almost as consistent an influence in shaping Christian memories as the written Gospels. Thus, for Christians, Easter is an annual event just as much as it is a narrative in writing. And Christmas may be even more a yearly occurrence than a nativity narrative.

What was the faith of the early church as witnessed to by its use of time? It was, above all else, faith in the Resurrection. Secondly, it was trust in the abiding presence of the Holy Spirit, known and experienced in the holy church. And it was belief that witnessed to those signs by which God had become manifest among us in Jesus Christ. This may not be a systematic summation of Christian belief; but it gives a clear indication of the heart of the faith of the early church, revealed by how it kept time.

There even was an implicitly Trinitarian structure: belief in the Father made manifest, the Son risen, and the Holy Spirit indwelling. This, however, should not be pushed too far. It is rather embarrassing to compare how the early church kept time through staunch testimony to God's activities and how the modern church keeps time with heavy concentration on its own programs and efforts. It will be helpful to probe deeper into how the early church kept time so that we may compare its practices with ours. Maybe we shall find some reasons to adjust our priorities to those of the heroic age of Christianity.

Our story begins not with the church year but the church week, particularly with the testimony of Sunday. And our story really begins with the first day of creation when "God said, 'Let there be light,' and there was light, . . . So evening came, and morning came, the first day" (Genesis 1:3-5). The Four Gospels are all careful to state that it was on the morning of the first day, i.e., the day on which creation had begun and the moment God had "separated light from darkness," that the empty tomb was discovered.

In at least three places the New Testament indicates a special time for worship, probably Sunday. Paul told the Christians in Corinth to set aside money for the collection on the first day of the week (I Corinthians 16:2). At Troas, after talking until midnight on Saturday, Paul broke bread and remained in conversation with Christians there until Sunday dawned (Acts 20:7 and 11). John tells us he "was caught up by the Spirit" and "it was on the Lord's day" (Revelation 1:10). The term "Lord's Day" had become a Christian term for the first day of the week by the early second century. Ignatius wrote about A.D. 115 to the Christians in Magnesia and spoke of those who "ceased to keep the [Jewish seventh day] Sabbath and lived by the Lord's Day, on which our life as well as theirs shone forth, thanks to Him and his death."[1] The *Didache*, written sometime in the late first or early second century, reminds Christians "on the Lord's day of the Lord come together, break bread and hold eucharist."[2] And even pagans noticed that "on an appointed day they [Christians] had been accustomed to meet before daybreak" though Pliny, the Roman administrator who wrote those words, hardly understood this meeting for the Lord's Supper.[3]

A new term appeared by the middle of the second century. Justin told his pagan audience about A.D. 155 that "we all hold this common gathering on Sunday since it is the first day, on which God transforming darkness and matter made the universe, and Jesus Christ our Savior rose from the dead on the same day."[4] Christians soon adopted the newly coined pagan term, "Sunday," and compared Christ's rising from the dead to the rising of the sun. Even

15

today, English and German speak of "Sunday," while French and Italian refer to the "Lord's Day." The *Epistle of Barnabas* called Sunday "an eighth day, that is the beginning of another world . . . in which Jesus also rose from the dead."[5] The themes of a new creation and light are important dimensions in the Christian celebration of Sunday as the day of the Resurrection.

Sunday was a day of worship but not of rest. It was made such by the Emperor Constantine in A.D. 321. "All judges, city people and craftsmen shall rest on the venerable day of the Sun. But countrymen may without hindrance attend to agriculture."[6]

The week had still more contour to it for the early church. Luke tells of the Pharisee who said, "I fast twice a week" (18:12). But the *Didache* told Christians: "Your fasts must not be identical with those of the hypocrites. They fast on Mondays and Thursdays; but you should fast on Wednesdays and Fridays."[7] The reasons are explained by a late fourth-century document, *The Apostolic Constitutions*. "Fast . . . on the fourth day of the week, . . . Judas then promising to betray Him for money; and . . . on [Friday] because on that day the Lord suffered the death of the cross."[8] There is evidence that some early Christians also held a certain regard for Saturday as "the memorial of the creation" from which work God rested on the seventh day. Tertullian tells us there were "some few who abstain from kneeling on the Sabbath" as on Sunday. But these other days were decidely inferior in importance compared with Sunday.

Sunday stood out because it was the weekly anniversary of the Resurrection. In the early church, Sunday also commemorated the Lord's passion, death, and resurrection; but it was above all the day on which the Savior rose from the dead. Even today, Sunday takes precedence over all other occasions. Sunday always witnesses to the risen Lord. It is the Lord's Day, the day of the sun risen from darkness, the start of the new creation. Tertullian tells us Christians did not kneel on Sunday, "the day of the Lord's resurrection." Sundays in Advent and Lent remain days of joy, though within penitential seasons. Each Sunday testifies to the resurrection faith. Sunday is a weekly little Easter above and beyond the yearly great Easter.

Even the day itself became for the early Church a structure of praise. The *Didache* instructed Christians to pray the Lord's Prayer three times a day. Psalm 55:17 spoke of calling upon God "evening and morning and at noon." Another psalm declared: "Seven times a day I praise thee for the justice of thy decrees" (119:164) and "at midnight I rise to give thee thanks" (62). By the early third century, Tertullian could speak of the third, sixth, and ninth hours of the day as times of "special solemnity in divine prayers" because of actions of the apostles at those times.

Hippolytus, an early third-century Roman Christian, could speak of seven daily occasions for prayer. For him nine A.M., noon, and three P.M., respectively, recalled the moments at which Christ was nailed to the cross, "There was a great darkness," and he died. Each day memorialized the crucifixion in this way. Hippolytus saw midnight as a time of prayer, for the bridegroom comes at midnight (Matthew 25:6), and we must be prepared to meet him. Prayer is needed at cockcrow, for at this moment Christ was denied (Matthew 26:75). Prayer is also advocated upon rising and retiring. Monasticism later developed the hours of the day into a daily eight-fold cycle of prayer. Chrysostom urged newly baptized Christians to begin each day's work with prayer for strength to do God's will and for everyone to end the day by rendering "an account to the Master of his whole day, and beg forgiveness for his falls."[9] The Christian day, then, early became a cycle of remembering Christ throughout one's daily labors in the midst of world concerns.

Just as the week and the day witnessed to Jesus Christ, so too, the early church saw the year as a structure for commemorating its Lord. Just as Sunday was the center of the week, so the year focused on the Pascha (Passover-Easter) happenings as its central feature. The Pascha was, in effect, a yearly Sunday. The Pascha had been the center of the Jewish year; it was no less so for Christians. Paul deliberately took over the language of the Jewish feast of unleavened bread (the Pascha):

> The old leaven of corruption is working among you. Purge it out, and then you will be bread of a new baking. As Christians you are unleavened Passover bread; for indeed our Passover has begun; the sacrifice is offered—Christ himself. So we who observe the festival must not use the old leaven, the leaven of corruption and wickedness, but only the unleavened bread which is sincerity and truth (I Corinthians 5:7-8).

It was the old Jewish event of deliverance but now made completely new in Jesus Christ. Slavery and redemption were rehearsed, but in a new sense through release from sin and death by what Christ had done.

The Early church kept the Pascha with services signifying the making of new Christians through the acts of baptism, confirmation, and first communion. Just as the Pascha commemorated the escape from slavery by passage through the Red Sea, so the church saw baptism as a burial with Christ in which "we were buried with him, and lay dead, in order that, as Christ was raised from the dead . . . we shall also be one with him in a resurrection like his" (Romans 6:4-5). In the earliest church, Christ's passion, death, and resurrection were commemorated together at the Pascha. Tertullian tells us that "the Passover affords a more than usually solemn day for baptism; when, withal, the Lord's passion in which we are baptized, was completed."[10] Hippolytus tells us that those to be baptized fasted on Friday and Saturday and then began an all-night vigil Saturday evening. At cockcrow at the hour of the Resurrection on Easter morning, they were baptized beneath the waters and rose with Christ as from the dead.

Early in the fourth century the church finally agreed that, unlike the Jewish Passover, the Pascha must always be celebrated on a Sunday. The Quartodeciman controversy clearly recognized the symbolic meaning of Sunday. "Never on any day other than the Lord's Day should the mystery of the Lord's resurrection from the dead be celebrated, . . . on that day alone we should observe the end of the Paschal fast."[11] Thus, the weekly and yearly cycle of resurrection reinforced each other.

In the course of the fourth century, the ancient unitive Pascha, which commemorated all the events of the last days of Jesus in Jerusalem, was divided into distinct commemorations. The dissolution apparently first occurred in Jerusalem where time and space came together at the holy sites. A need was felt to hold separate commemorations for each event at the holy places in order to serve the throngs of pilgrims who were arriving from all over the world. Scripture itself was mined for evidence as to time and place of all the events of Christ's last week in Jerusalem. We have a good example of what had developed by about A.D. 384 as chronicled in the writings of a Spanish woman named Egeria. Her notes, apparently written down so she could give talks when she got back home, have survived and give us a clear insight as to how late fourth-century Jerusalem had developed its way of keeping time. These developments in Jerusalem have shaped Christian practice ever since.

Egeria tells us that Palm/Passion Sunday "is the beginning of the Easter Week or, as they call it here, 'The Great Week.' . . . All the people go before him [the bishop] with psalms and antiphons, all the time repeating, 'Blessed is he that cometh in the name of the Lord.' " [12] There were minor services on the next three days, except that on Wednesday the presbyter reads about Judas' plot to betray Jesus, and "the people groan and lament at this reading." On Thursday, after everyone has received Communion, all "conduct the bishop to Gethsemane." And on Friday, services occur on Golgotha where fragments of the wood of the cross are adored by all the people who process past the cross and kiss it. By the end of the century, Augustine states that "it is clear from the Gospel on what days the Lord was crucified and rested in the tomb and rose again" and that the church has "a requirement of retaining those same days."[13] The ancient unitive Pascha had been broken into separate commemorations: Maundy Thursday, Good Fri-

19

day, and the Easter Vigil, plus Palm/Passion Sunday and the three lesser days of Holy Week. And this is how we have kept it ever since. This gives us Holy Week beginning with Palm/Passion Sunday, Monday, Tuesday, (Spy) Wednesday, Maundy Thursday, Good Friday, Holy Saturday, and Easter (Eve and Day). The English term "Easter" comes from the Old English "Eastre," a pagan spring festival; romance languages use forms of "Pascha."

Closely connected with Easter are two seasons, Lent and Easter. Lent began as a period of preparation for those who had been set apart after considerable preparation as catechumens before being baptized at the Easter Vigil. The Council of Nicaea, A.D. 325, first referred to Lent as "forty days." About A.D. 348, Bishop Cyril of Jerusalem told those about to be baptized, "You have a long period of grace, forty days for repentence."[14] By Augustine's time Lent had become a time of preparation for all Christians, baptized or not, in that "part of the year . . . adjoining . . . and touching on the Lord's passion."

Far more important was the Easter Season, the fifty days extending the celebration of Easter through the Day of Pentecost. The great fifty (the Pentecost) was far more important than the forty days of Lent. It is perplexing why modern Christians concentrate on Lent, the season of sorrow, rather than on the Easter Season, the season of joy. Augustine tells us: "These days after the Lord's Resurrection form a period, not of labor, but of peace and joy. That is why there is no fasting and we pray standing, which is a sign of resurrection. This practice is observed at the altar on all Sundays, and the Alleluia is sung, to indicate that our future occupation is to be no other than the praise of God."[15] Easter then, was a day of the week, a day of the year, and a season. There can be no doubt as to the centrality of the Resurrection in the life and faith of the early church.

Second in importance was the celebration of another event, the Day of Pentecost. Like the Pascha, it was also a Jewish feast. "The day after the seventh sabbath will make fifty days, and then you shall present to the Lord a grain-offering from the new crop" (Leviticus 23:16).

Sometime during the first century, the Day of Pentecost came to reflect for Jews the giving of the law at Mt. Sinai. Paul contrasts this with the giving of the Spirit. "The law, then, engraved letter by letter upon stone, dispensed death, and yet it was inaugurated with divine splendour . . . . Must not even greater splendour rest upon the divine dispensation of the Spirit?" (II Corinthians 3:7-8). For Christians, that Day of Pentecost commemorated the birthday of the church when, with the noise of a wind, tongues of flame rested on the disciples, and they began to talk in other tongues to be understood (Acts 2:1-41). The book of Acts is a chronicle of the work of the Spirit-filled church in its earliest years.

Pentecost began as an unitive feast, too. Tertullian suggests that Christ had ascended into heaven at Pentecost.[16] And in the first half of the fourth century Eusebius speaks of "the august and holy solemnity of Pentecost, which is distinguished by a period of seven weeks, and sealed with that one day on which the holy Scriptures attest the ascension of our common Savior into heaven, and the descent of the Holy Spirit."[17] In other words, for almost four centuries, the Day of Pentecost commemorated both the ascension of Christ and the descent of the Holy Spirit. By the end of the fourth century, these two commemorations had been separated. The *Apostolic Constitutions* describes forty days after Easter as the proper time to "celebrate the feast of the ascension of the Lord." Once again, the biblical witness has been historicized. In this case, Acts 1:3 and its mention of "a period of forty days" during which Jesus taught his disciples seems to have been the source of pinpointing the date of the Ascension. Where there had been one feast, by the late fourth century there were two: Ascension and Pentecost. Christ was in heaven, and the Holy Spirit dwelt in the holy church on earth. It was a daily reality the church could experience, not an abstraction.

The third chief event in the calendar of the early church was the Epiphany. Its origins are more obscure; they were certainly not Jewish but probably were Egyptian. The date,

January 6, took the place of a pagan feast at the Egyptian winter solstice. The Epiphany signified several things, all of which had to do with the beginnings of Jesus Christ's work of manifesting God. This feast referred to the birth of Christ (with which two Gospels begin), to the baptism of Jesus (with which the other Gospels begin), and to the first miracle of which John's Gospel says: "This deed at Cana-in-Galilee is the first of the signs by which Jesus revealed [ephanérosen] his glory and led his disciples to believe in him" (2:11). The common theme of all these events is Jesus Christ manifesting God to humans. Appropriately, the early church often called this day "The Theophany" (manifestation of God) and some Eastern Orthodox churches still do. The prologue to the Fourth Gospel sets the theme: "God's only Son, he who is nearest to the Father's heart, he has made him known" (1:18).

Epiphany underwent a split in the first half of the fourth century, probably beginning in Rome. Our earliest mention of the new feast, Christmas, occurs in a document from A.D. 354, which reflects usage of about A.D. 336. It lists December 25 as *natus Christus in Betleem Iudeae*. Apparently this date was chosen to replace a pagan festival of the unconquered sun as the sun begins to wax again at the winter solstice. (By the fourth century, the Julian calendar was off by four days.) Gradually, the new festival of Christmas took over part of the commemorations of the Epiphany. Chrysostom told a congregation in Antioch on Christmas Day, A.D. 386: "This day . . . has now been brought to us, not many years ago, has developed so quickly and borne such fruit."[18] The following Epiphany Day he explained: "For this is the day on which he was baptized, and made holy the nature of the waters . . . . Why then is this the day called Epiphany? Because it was not when he was born that he became manifest to all, but when he was baptized; for up to this day he was unknown to the multitudes."[19]

The Epiphany, then is older than Christmas and has a deeper meaning. For instead of simply being an anniversary of the birth of Christ, it testifies to the whole purpose of the Incarnation: the manifestation of God in Jesus Christ, beginning both with his birth and with the beginning of his ministry (the baptism when he is proclaimed "My Son, my Beloved"). And the mighty signs and teachings, narrated in the gospels as Jesus accomplished this manifestation, make the Season after the Epiphany the commemoration of all those things which Jesus did up to the final events in Jerusalem.

A council in Spain in A.D. 380 decreed that "from December 17 until the day of Epiphany which is January 6 no one is permitted to be absent from Church."[20] This precedent for Advent dates from when Christmas, itself, was as yet unknown in Spain. By the fifth century, a forty-day season of preparation for the Epiphany was being practiced in Gaul (this paralleled Lent and began about when Advent now begins). Rome eventually adopted a four-week Advent before Christmas.

A process similar to that which had splintered the Pascha into a series of commemorations also operated with Christmas. As a Jewish boy, Jesus would likely have been circumcised and named on the eighth day after his birth. Luke tells us, "Eight days later the time came to circumcise him, and he was given the name Jesus" (2:21). Accordingly the commemoration on January 1 became known as the Feast of the Circumcision or the Name of Jesus. Luke 2:22-40 gives the story of the Presentation in the Temple, an event forty days after his birth, or February 2. It was discerned that the Annunciation mentioned in Luke 1:26-38 would have occurred nine months before Christmas, or March 25. Elizabeth was then six months pregnant, and Mary's subsequent visitation to Elizabeth (recorded in verses 39-56) was fixed at May 31, or just before the birth of John the Baptist, identified as June 24 (three months after the Annunciation). John's birth came at the summer solstice when the sun wanes until the birth of Christ. "As he grows greater, I must grow less" (John 3:30). All these developments are a combination of Luke 1 and 2 and obstetrics.

The Christian year, and especially the temporal cycle

(movable dates plus the Christmas cycle), was basically complete by the end of the fourth century. The subsequent history is that of development of the sanctoral cycle (those fixed dates commemorating the deaths of saints aside from dates based on Christmas). These began early; the "Martyrdom of Polycarp" mentions commemoration of a second-century martyr. Basically these were commemorations of local heroes and heroines of the faith. Tertullian tells us, "As often as the anniversary comes round, we make offerings for the dead as birthday honours,"[21] After all, one's birth into eternity (death) was far more important than his or her birth into time. The calendar increasingly became cluttered with commemorations of saints, especially after relics of saints began to be moved from place to place. Local saints eventually were supplemented by saints from other regions. Complications of the sanctoral cycle increasingly obscured the primitive temporal cycle.

Only two significant additions occurred after the fourth century: Trinity Sunday and All Saints' Day. Trinity Sunday, the Sunday after the Day of Pentecost, was introduced about A.D. 1000. Unlike other feasts, it represents a theological doctrine unrelated to an historical event. The ninth century saw the designation of November 1 as All Saints' Day. It had earlier springtime precedents, but the Gallican placement of it in the harvest season was accepted by Rome about A.D. 835.

Let us recapitulate. John Chrysostom, in a sermon preached in A.D. 386, effectively sums up the church's year of grace: "For if Christ had not been born into flesh, he would not have been baptized, which is the Theophany [Epiphany], he would not have been crucified [some texts add: and risen] which is the Pascha, he would not have sent down the Spirit, which is the Pentecost."[22] In the fourth century, the three great primitive feasts—the Epiphany, the Pascha, and the Day of Pentecost—had split from them related days—Christmas, Good Friday, and Ascension. Some have interpreted those divisions as a sign that the fourth-century church was becoming reconciled to time and was losing its fervent expectation of the end of time.

But this reconciliation to time was probably an inevitable process as those of us who have lived through a national bicentennial can attest. People want to know, to visualize, to experience for themselves. And so what happened in the fourth century was a dramatic way of expressing the central realities the church experienced—manifestation, resurrection, and the indwelling Spirit. Eschatological fervor did slacken with the peace of the church after Constantine. But the imagination of Christians directed backward in time was no less fruitful and intensified their perception of the Incarnation. The success of these fourth-century changes is shown by their vivid presence among us even today. Obviously they have rung true to both Christian faith and human experience.

All in all, the church year is very satisfactory reflection of the life and faith of the early church and has remained in use with little change ever since. Modern efforts to systematize and tidy it up have never been satisfactory. Granted the ancient church year leaves large gaps in time, especially after the Day of Pentecost. But its strength lies in its firm grasp of the core of the Christian experience and in its ability to reflect in a vivid way that Christ has made God manifest, that Christ has risen from the dead, and that Christ has sent the Holy Spirit to dwell in the holy church.

The sixteenth-century reformers took various approaches to the calendar. Luther purified it of saints' day's by seeking "to celebrate only on Lord's Days and on Festivals of the Lord, abrogating completely the festivals of all the saints. . . . We regard the Festivals of the Purification [Presentation] and of the Annunciation as Festivals of Christ, like the Epiphany and the Circumcision."[23] The Church of England originally only retained materials to commemorate saints mentioned in the Bible plus All Saints' Day. The Church of Scotland was more radical. Its 1560 *Book of Discipline* condemned all "feasts (as they term them) of apostles, martyrs, virgins, of Christmas, circumcision, epiphany, purification, and other fond feasts of our Lady. Which things, because in God's Scriptures they neither have commandment nor assurance, we judge utterly to be abolished from this realm; affirming further, that the obstinate maintainers and teachers of such abominations ought not to escape the punishment of the civil magistrate."[24] John Wesley, always the pragmatist, abolished "most of the holy-days . . . as at present answering no valuable end."[25] His calendar included the four Sundays of Advent, Christmas-day, up to fifteen Sundays after Christmas, the Sunday next before Easter, Good-Friday, Easter-Day, five Sundays after Easter, Ascension-day, Sunday after Ascension-day, Whit-Sunday, Trinity Sunday, and up to twenty-five Sundays after Trinity. His journals reveal a personal fondness for All Saints' Day (cf. p. 109). Both Wesley's calendar and lections were soon lost among American Methodists.

Renewed interest in the church year among American Protestants occurred in the 1920s and 30s, a period in which an aesthetic approach to worship tended to be prominent. An effort to rearrange the year was advanced in the form of a new season, Kingdomtide. It seems to have been promoted largely by Fred Winslow Adams of Boston University School of Theology. Kingdomtide originally appeared in a Federal Council of Churches publication, The Christian Year, published in 1937 and 1940. The first edition suggested observing Kingdomtide for the last six months of the church year; in 1940 this time was divided between Whitsuntide and Kingdomtide.[26] Eventually only Methodists were left observing Kingdomtide, and the new United Methodist calendar omits it. A somewhat similar experiment was briefly tried by American Presbyterians. They experimented with a suggestion made in 1956 by Allan McArthur, a Scottish pastor, of having a season of God the Father[27] in the fall. After four years of trial use, this, too, was abandoned.

Since Vatican II there has emerged a profound new interest in the calendar and a deep new appreciation of how the way we keep time shapes and reflects our lives as Christians. The first landmark was the new Roman Calendar, which went into effect among Roman Catholics on the first day of the 1970s. It represents the most careful scrutiny ever attempted of the way Christians use time. Most of its reforms have been adopted by the major Protestant bodies in this country: Lutherans, Episcopalians, Presbyterians, the United Church of Christ, the Christian Church (Disciples of Christ), and (as an alternative calendar) United Methodists.

The most radical Catholic change, that of not treating the weeks after the Epiphany or the Day of Pentecost as distinct seasons but only as parts of the "Season of the year," has not been adopted by Protestants. But the other basic changes have. The Lutheran practice of commemorating the Sunday before Ash Wednesday as Sunday of the Transfiguration of the Lord has been accepted by Episcopalians and United Methodists as well. For the first time in four hundred years, we have a genuinely ecumenical calendar followed by the vast majority of Christians in this country. The newest calendar is the result of a careful attempt to recapture the structure and meaning of the oldest calendar, that of the early church. It is to be hoped that this calendar will prove a strong witness among us to the chief priorities of Christian faith.

Theology of Keeping Time

How the church kept time in early centuries had been discussed in detail because, as so often happens in Christian worship, if we understand well the experiences of the church's first three centuries, little further information is necessary. It will be worthwhile, though, to reflect a bit on the meaning of what we have covered.

It is revealing to compare the keeping of time in the early church with current practice. We may see a shocking contrast. The average congregation today finds its time occupied with various promotions much like the calendar of a department store. Instead of a white sale or Washington's birthday sale, we have our own array of loyalty Sundays, rally days, student recognition Sundays, etc. Even the seasons have been misinterpreted. Until recently a narrow view of Epiphany was prevalent. The

United Methodist *Book of Hymns* places missions under Epiphany with such hymns as "Heralds of Christ" or "We've a Story to Tell to the Nations." And Kingdomtide all too often carries the suggestion that the kingdom will be brought in by the exertion of greater effort on our part. The hymn "Turn Back, O Man" reflects this optimism in resolute human effort.

All these aspects of the modern de facto calendar betray one great difference from that of the early church. *Our de facto calendar stresses human agency; that of the early church depended entirely upon what God had done and continues to do through the Holy Spirit.* Our keeping of time has a strongly humanistic tint. We cannot quite let God do it all for us. We even worry about whether we feel the right things at Christmas and Easter. Yet the point of the church's year of grace is that all is done for us. All we have to do is to accept what God has done. Then we really are free to act. The church's year is one that at once recognizes the futility of our efforts and yet exults in God's victories.

In short, the church year is a constant reminder of gifts that we cannot create but only accept. Pius Parsch called it the church's year of grace.[28] Throughout the year we are reminded that salvation is a gift offered to us in all its different aspects by the various seasons and special days. Humanizing the year by making it a recital of our own activities misses the point altogether. Focusing on particular promotional causes instead of God's actions is a constant pressure that has to be resisted. Yet, unfortunately, the promotional level seems to be the favorite way of keeping time for many congregations. If our de facto calendar truly witnesses to our faith, it is an impoverished faith indeed that we manifest. It suggests that faith in our efforts and activities rather than in God's.

Recovery of the church year can help us sort out for ourselves our real priorities. Keeping time with the rhythms of the early church can be a real source of renewal for us today. It can help us see the woods from the trees.

In briefest terms, the church year functions to show forth Jesus Christ until he comes again, and to testify to God the

Holy Spirit indwelling the church in the meantime. The church year is both proclamation and thanksgiving. In much the same way as Jewish and Christian prayer recite what we give thanks for, so the Christian year proclaims and thanks God for God's marvelous actions. Christians and Jews praise God, not in abstract terms, but by reciting the marvelous works of God. It is a think/thank process by which we glorify God through recalling what God has done. Thus the Christian year reflects the very nature of Christian prayer and our relationship to God. Much of its power, as with daily prayer, comes through reiteration. Year after year, week after week, day by day, the acts of God are commemorated and our apprehension of them deepened. These cycles save us from a false spirituality, based on ourselves, by showing forth God's works instead.

Keeping time, of course, can also become an idolatrous gimmick like anything else that is good. Time can be used simply to dress up our services and to make them look fashionable. Keeping the church year for the wrong reasons is worse than useless for we can end up worshiping our own gimmicks rather than God. But when we do use the structures of time to bring us closer to God they can serve that purpose exceedingly well.

How does it bring us closer to God? The church year is a means by which we relive for ourselves all that matters of salvation history. When we recall the past events of salvation, they come alive in their present power to save. The doing of acts of remembrance brings the original events back to us with all their meaning. And so we continue to "proclaim the death of the Lord, until he comes" (I Corinthians 11:26). Acts of proclaiming the Lord's death gives us the benefits of his death. The various acts of rehearsing all of salvation history gives us anew the power of these past events. Christ's birth, baptism, death, resurrection, etc. are all given to us for our own appropriation through corporate re-enactment of them. These events become no longer simply detached data from the past but part of our own personal history as we relive salvation history through rehearsing it in our worship.

Thus Christ dies again in our consciousness every Good Friday. And every Easter and Lord's Day we are witnesses to the Resurrection.

The Christian year becomes a vital and refreshing means through which God is given to us. It is a giving that is never exhausted. Each time the year, week, and day push us a bit deeper into encounter with God. We perceive one aspect of Christ submitting to baptism this year, another next year, but never do we touch bottom. So the year is a constant means of grace through which we receive God's gifts to us.

It is important to remember that the year is about what God does for us, not our gifts to God. The whole structure calls attention to God's work, not to ours. And God's work is made known in the changing events and needs of each time and place.

Advent is both a time of thanks for the gift of Christ to us in past time and anticipation of his second coming. It contains both threat and promise. Christmas rehearses God's self-giving in the birth of Jesus Christ. The Christmas Season comes to a strong conclusion in the Epiphany.

The Season after the Epiphany has been sadly neglected. The whole season stresses the various ways in which Jesus Christ has made God manifest to us by making the Father known through mighty signs and teachings. These begin with Christ's baptism (when his sonship is declared and his ministry begins). They continue with recital of the signs and teachings by which he made his glory known through manifesting God. The season ends with the Last Sunday after the Epiphany, or the Transfiguration of the Lord, in which Christ is once again proclaimed, "My Son, my Beloved."

Lent is the season in which we anticipate that final trip to Jerusalem and the self-giving nature of love shown in Christ's passion and death. All is changed as Christ gives himself to us as the resurrected one at Easter. The Easter Season begins with Easter Eve and comes to a strong finish on the Day of Pentecost.

The Season after Pentecost signals the long interim of the new covenant church until he comes again. The Last

Sunday after Pentecost or Christ the King pushes us to anticipate the consummation of all things when Christ comes again in glory as King of all and all human failures and achievements are, at last, made of no account.

The minor christological feasts have evangelical values that we are just beginnng to discover. The Name of Jesus, Presentation, Annunciation, and Visitation are all christological and call attention to Christ's full humanity and his identification with our social patterns. All Saints' Day is christological, too. It does not dwell on the virtues of the saints but on the love of Christ who works in his people throughout time to accomplish his purposes. The chief value of commemorating the saints is recognition through them of Christ who never leaves us. If commemoration of individual saints could help us realize this, such piety could once again serve a "valuable end."

Operating Instructions

Every service of Christian worship is composed of two kinds of acts of worship: ordinary and proper. The ordinary elements are those which remain the same from week to week: the basic structure of the service, the Lord's Prayer, the offering, possibly a creed, a doxology, a prayer of confession, a benediction, etc. The proper parts are those elements that change from week to week. We read different lessons, sing varied hymns, pray a variety of prayers, and hear (it is hoped) a somewhat different sermon each time we gather for worship.

Our concerns in this book are not with the ordinary parts. They are dealt with thoroughly in *Word and Table*[29] and in *Companion to the Book of Worship*.[30] Anyone using the resources in this book should certainly be familiar with *Word and Table*, especially the "Basic Pattern of Worship" on pages 8-11. If that basic pattern is followed, the materials in this book will be much more useful, and our worship will have much more functional clarity than is often the case. The structure of worship is extremely important, but it is not the concern of this book.

The importance of the *proper parts* in Christian worship is that they supply variety and interest. While the ordinary parts provide a necessary constancy, Christian worship without the proper parts would be deadly dull, a repetition of the same thing week after week. Without the constants that the ordinary parts provide, Christian worship would be chaos.

Variety is an important ingredient in Christian worship. The good news of the gospel is much too wide and deep to be encompassed by a single service or season. Every time the congregation gathers for worship is a different event. Never before and never again will exactly the same people be assembled for worship. But the uniqueness of each gathering goes beyond that. The life of the local community, as well as the national and global communities, is never the same from week to week. Christian worship reflects this in its acknowledgment that every Sunday or special day is a different occasion, and it encourages this diversity. Christmas is not Easter nor the Sunday after Easter the same as the Sunday before Labor Day, though the attendance may be about the same. A wedding is not a funeral, though the flowers may be similar. Nor is a Sunday evening service the same occasion as that morning's service, for the people may be in a more relaxed mood in the evening. In a similar way, no two family meals are identical. Each occasion for worship is unique.

Variety, then, is a basic characteristic of Christian worship as it relates to both the eternal gospel and our ongoing daily life. One of the sharpest criticisms of Christian worship in recent years has been its dullness. Yet this criticism is apt only when Christian worship has been unfaithful to its own nature. The surest way to avoid the dullness of repetition is to revel in the rich variety that Christian worship makes possible. And the best way to insure dullness is to ignore the rich variety that Christian worship provides.

Nothing is a better source for variety and interest in Christian worship than careful following of the church year. The structure of the year provides an orderly pegboard on which to hang all our best ideas and is a real creative stimulus. The first question to raise when planning any service ought to be: "When does it occur in the church year?" The answer should be our first and best clue due to providing ideas. The church year divides the fullness of the gospel into digestible fragments so we have enough to savor afresh each week of the year.

The calendar is the basis of Christian worship. The reader will probably want to refer to it frequently as he or she reads what follows. The calendar printed as chapter 1 is the new alternative calendar adopted by The United Methodist Church in November of 1974 and developed in conjunction with other denominations through the Consultation on Church Union. Others may prefer to follow the calendar on pages 62 to 64 of the *Book of Worship*. The differences between them are relatively slight with the exception of Kingdomtide. The *Book of Worship* has that season; the new calendar does not. United Methodists are free to use either method. It is quite possible to observe the new calendar and also keep Kingdomtide from the last Sunday of August until Advent. The *Book of Worship* calls the sixth season Pentecost; the new calendar labels it the Season after Pentecost.

How does the new calendar work? It consists of sixty-seven possible occasions arranged in six seasons: Advent, Christmas Season, the Season after the Epiphany, Lent, Easter Season, and the Season after Pentecost. For purposes of convenience, in the resources that follow each occasion is given a number from the First Sunday in Advent (1) to All Saints' Day (67). Not all sixty-seven occasions occur in any year due to the varying lengths of the Season after the Epiphany and the Season after Pentecost. The number of Sundays in Advent, Lent, and the Easter Season are constants. It is important to remember that rarely are all the Sundays after the Epiphany used. The final Sunday of this season (that just prior to Ash Wednesday) is always number seventeen, the Last Sunday after the Epiphany or the Transfiguration of the Lord. The same is true after Pentecost; the Sunday

33

before the beginning of Advent is always number sixty-six, Last Sunday after Pentecost or Christ the King.

It may help to remember that each season except Advent begins and ends with a special day. The Christmas Season extends from Christmas Eve and Day through the Epiphany, the Season after the Epiphany from the Baptism of the Lord through the Transfiguration of the Lord, Lent from Ash Wednesday through Saturday of Holy Week, the Easter Season from Easter Vigil and Day through the Day of Pentecost, and the Season after Pentecost from Trinity through Christ the King. Note that white is used on all these special days except for those in Advent and Lent and the Day of Pentecost.

A few other dates are new to us or have special problems. Epiphany Day may be celebrated on the first Sunday of January. If that comes on January 1, the resources could be combined with those for the First Sunday after Christmas, or, if it comes on January 7, with those for the Baptism of the Lord. If Christmas is on a Sunday, we may use the resources for the First Sunday after Christmas, especially if the Christmas materials have been used on Christmas Eve.

The Baptism of the Lord is a new festival for Western Christians. Baptism of the Lord comes on the first Sunday after January 6 (the Epiphany). Palm/Passion Sunday is now regarded as one and the same, since this is when the passion narrative is usually read as provided in the new lectionary. The Easter Vigil ought to be celebrated the eve before Easter Day or during that night. And Ascension Day may be commemorated on the Seventh Sunday of Easter, if deemed wise. The Day of Pentecost has recovered its earlier place as the fiftieth day and last Sunday of the Easter Season, the season once known as Pentecost. All Saints Day may be observed on the first Sunday of November when November 1 is not a Sunday.

It will be necessary to exercise discretion with regard to promotional, patriotic, and other topical occasions. Never should Mothers' Day, for instance, take precedence over the Day of Pentecost though one can make discrete references to motherhood on Pentecost Day, if considered necessary. Thanksgiving Day certainly has religious overtones. Though not listed in the calendar, it is often observed with ecumenical and inter-religious services. *Word and Table* suggests the following resources for Thanksgiving Day: Psalms 65, 95, 96 (*Book of Hymns*, 575 or 607), Deuteronomy 8:7-18, II Corinthians 9:6-12, and Luke 12:16-31.

For those who would like to keep the minor christological feasts there are other possibilities. The color for each is usually white. The Name of Jesus (January 1) calls to mind Jesus's humanity and his full identification with human society. Most appropriate is Psalm 8 (*Book of Hymns*, 555), Numbers 6:22-27, Romans 1:1-7, and Luke 2:15-21. Presentation (February 2) traditionally was called Purification, or Candlemas, since the candles to be used that year were blessed on this occasion. It can call attention to the aged in our society who, Luke tells us, were the first to proclaim the Lord (Anna and Simeon). Suggested resources include: Psalm 84 (*Book of Hymns*, 579), Malachi 3:1-4, Hebrews 2:14-18, and Luke 2:22-40. Annunciation—Lady Day in some countries—(March 25) calls attention to the power of the humblest person when fulfilling God's will. Psalm 40 (*Book of Hymns*, 568) is appropriate and Isaiah 7:10-14, Hebrews 10:4-10, and Luke 1:26-38. Visitation (May 31), with its dialogue between two women, calls attention to the Incarnation and contains Mary's song, the *Magnificat*, in essence the social creed of Christianity. Appropriate resources include Psalm 113 and Zephaniah 3:14-18a, Romans 12:9-16, and Luke 1:39-56 (*Book of Hymns*, 612). However, the course of the normal Sunday readings ought not be broken without good reason since the lessons are constructed to cover all portions of Scripture.

If the calendar is the foundation of the structure of Christian worship, the first floor is certainly the lectionary based on the Christian year. One of the most significant changes in United Methodist worship in recent years has been the widespread adoption of the new lectionary and the use of it as the basis of preaching in thousands of congregations. All too often previous haphazard methods of choosing scripture had, in fact, eliminated major portions of God's Word and reshaped scripture in our own image. Social activists might be partial to passages in the prophetic books and conservatives to the more rigid passages in the pastoral epistles. Yet both, in choosing passages they found congenial, were, in effect, rewriting scripture. Liberals and conservatives were equally guilty of revising God's Word in accord with personal preferences.

One of the most useful results of the post-Vatican II era has been the development of an ecumenical lectionary. Begun after Vatican II by the Roman Catholic Church, several years' work by a full-time staff and eight hundred consultants—Protestants, Catholics, and Jews—brought it to its present form. For Roman Catholics it went into effect with the beginning of the 1970 liturgical year on November 30, 1969. It is the most carefully prepared lectionary in all Christian history. United Methodists began using it as an alternative lectionary on December 1, 1974, after having worked on the Consultation on Church Union in preparing a consensus of the Roman Catholic, Episcopalian, Presbyterian, and Lutheran versions. These churches, as well as the United Church of Christ and the Christian Church (Disciples of Christ), now use it too. It is the most widely used lectionary in American history.

How does it work? There are lections for each of the sixty-seven dates in the new United Methodist calendar. These will be found, numbered in sequence, in the resources section of this book. The new lectionary is a three-year lectionary, the years designated as A, B, and C. Year C is a year, such as a 1980, evenly divisible by the number 3. The church year begins between November 27 and December 3 of the preceding civil year so that Advent in civil year December, 1979 is part of the church year 1980 and hence is year C.

For each Sunday three lessons are appointed: first (usually Old Testament), second (usually an Epistle), and Gospel. During the Easter Season, lessons from the book of Acts are read as the story of the new creation begins with the Resurrection. Chrysostom explains that the book of Acts is "the demonstration of the Resurrection" and hence is read during the Season after Easter, a custom which Augustine also notes in Africa. Occasionally Revelation takes the place of the Epistle. In the course of three years, most of the New Testament and large portions of the Old Testament are read when all three lessons are used. Two principles are in operation here. The Gospels reflect the church year with the first lessons more or less dependent upon them. The second lessons, on the other hand, are usually read in order from each book from beginning to end. First Corinthians, for example, is read chiefly during the Epiphany Season. Year A is devoted to reading the Gospel of Matthew; year B to Mark; and Year C to Luke. Portions in all three years are filled in from the Fourth Gospel. The new lectionary provides the most comprehensive method of reading the entire Bible, one that can be accomplished in three years. Then it is time to start over again. There are two exceptional dates: On Palm/Passion Sunday the full passion narrative may be read, especially in dramatic fashion. For the Easter Vigil, the traditional scheme of nine lessons with their marvelously rich Old Testament imagery is suggested.

More than any single item, the lectionary guides the choices appropriate to us on any given Sunday. It is reflected in the opening prayer, the psalm, the hymns, the choral and instrumental music, the sermon, and the visual materials used. The second question to ask in planning any service is "What does the lectionary provide?" The use of a lectionary makes it possible to plan actual services months or even years in advance. This makes it especially useful for musicians and artists who need much advance preparation. Since the lectionary shapes other choices, it is important that we examine briefly its effect on them in turn.

An opening prayer is sometimes an effective way to articulate the general thrust of the lessons for the day and alert the congregation to the event. Those given in the resources section that follows include some for special occasions: weddings, funerals, etc. Some are provided that might be for occasional use during entire shorter seasons. Those appropriate for a special day are included on that date. They are all meant to be succinct summations of the event at hand and should be an incentive for others to write similar prayers. They represent an adaptation of the ancient collect form to modern use.

The Psalms have often been the most neglected part of United Methodist worship and among the dreariest. Included in chapter 3 are psalms chosen for each year on all sixty-seven events. Thus they make available a much wider selection of psalms than Methodists have ever used. Unfortunately, the present *Book of Hymns* only includes fifty-seven psalms, and most of these are fragments. Paperback psalters in a variety of translations can be purchased for pew use or pew Bibles used. With them the full range of the Psalms can be regained. Failing this, numbers of the psalms in the *Book of Hymns* are given. That means the same psalms must be used each year. The psalms are chosen deliberately to relate to the lessons provided. Obviously, this works better with the greater selection a full psalter makes possible. A psalm is a response, and does not function as a lesson. It needs to be matched carefully to the lessons.

A hymn lectionary is also provided in chapter 3. Possible hymns are suggested for each occasion. Those interested in exploring hymns not in the *Book of Hymns* should consult *Lessons and Hymns*, published by the Baltimore Annual Conference. Write the Section on Worship, Board of Discipleship, PO Box 840, Nashville, Tennessee 37202 for further information.

No one has ever questioned that J. S. Bach wrote some of the greatest of all church music while following the guidance of the lectionary and calendar. Too often we fail to sense how successfully choral music can mesh with the ministry of the word by providing a musical commentary on the lessons. Frequently anthems unrelated to the occasion intrude into the carefully planned sequence of the service. This is not at all necessary. Careful use of the calendar and lectionary can be a tremendous boon to church musicians, and ministers, especially since it gives them lead time to order and rehearse appropriate music. The same applies also to instrumental music.

Nothing is as thoroughly and obviously affected by the lessons as is the sermon, or at least we would hope so. There seem to be three main results from the widespread use of the new lectionary. It has made it financially feasible to publish a number of top-quality aids to biblical study in the form of commentaries and other resources to improve our use of the Bible. For a current list of these, write the Section on Worship, PO Box 840, Nashville, Tennessee 37202. Second, the lectionary has forced us to preach on a much wider selection of scripture than most of us did. That does not mean that one should preach on all three lessons at one time. Sometimes they relate to each other well; sometimes they go their own separate ways. But to preach on any one of these texts will force us to study and ponder many portions of God's Word that are unfamiliar to us. And third, if we really follow the year and the lessons carefully, we find ourselves probing deeper into Christology. One simply cannot preach on the Baptism of the Lord, the Transfiguration, Palm/Passion Sunday, All Saints' Day, and the like, without being forced to make up our minds about whom we say Jesus Christ is. Without such discipline, it is amazing how long we can jump around that vital question. Many preachers have agreed that preaching from the lectionary improves the content of their preaching. And many have been amazed how relevant assigned passages often are for the congregation's time and place.

Finally, we must say a word on the visual aspects of the lectionary and calendar. We have largely been blind to these matters. One could go to church week after week, and it looked as if all times and occasions for worship were identical. But now our eyes have been opened. We have realized that the gospel can be seen as well as heard. One church used a banner showing a tow-headed boy blowing a whistle and the words, "God so loved the world . . . well you would hardly believe it!" How many sermons have we heard and forgot about John 3:16? But memory of that banner will remain for years.

Ideally we ought to have a different building each Sunday. The amazing thing is that it is possible to a certain extent. With the use of textiles, graphics, and other art forms we can have a new church setting each Sunday, just as the whole appearance of a living room is changed by adding some orange pillows on the davenport. And where projections are possible, a wall can be whatever we want to project on it. "Okay, we'll have the Sistine Chapel this week, but for next week's lesson Big Sur would work better." We are limited only by the horizons of our imaginations.

Some of the things we have learned about worship in the last few years seem irrevocable. In 1966 few, if any, United Methodist churches had ever used a banner. By now, few have not. If the gospel can be proclaimed visually, why shouldn't it be? Each new dimension we add to our perception of the good news seems to be clear gain.

How do we do it? The simplest concept is just using pure color. Color helps form general expectations for any occasion. We don't wear flamboyant colors to a funeral. Traditionally purples, greys, and blues have been used for seasons of a penitential character such as Advent and Lent. White has been used for events and seasons with a strong christological flavor, such as Christmas or the Baptism of the Lord. Red has been reserved for occasions relating to the Holy Spirit, such as the Day of Pentecost, or to commemorations of martyrs. Green has been used for seasons of less pronounced character such as the Season after the Epiphany or the Season after Pentecost. These longer seasons need not stagnate in a single color or hue any more than nature retains a monotonous green as the delicate shades of spring progress to the deeper hues of fall.

Much may be done with pure color. However, we are coming to realize the need to be equally sensitive to hues and textures. A silk purple might be less preferable for Lent than a rough-textured blue or gray. And a splendid gold might be better for Easter than a rough white material.

Colors and textures can be used most effectively in textiles for hangings on pulpits, lecterns (if any), the stoles worn by ordained ministers, or ministerial vestments. Sometimes bolts of cloth may simply be hung as giant abstract banners. It is better not to hide the altar-table with cloth hangings since a simple white table cloth expresses its function better.

Banners can be hung almost anywhere in the church. Increasingly we see a move to large-scale banners, fifteen feet in length or so. They ought to be changed frequently as the year turns. The Easter church building ought to be quite different from the Lenten church.

Posters, bulletins, placards, and other graphic forms can express the gospel in forceful ways. Photographs may be blown up cheaply. A few words of press type—"Lord, when was it that we saw you?" (Matthew 25:37) or "Is it of no concern to you who pass by?" (Lamentations 1:12)—lettered on them may be a powerful message. Try to discover key words for any occasion—"Peace on earth"; "My Son"; "He is risen"—and use them. Visit a local art supply store to see how many possibilities we have neglected. Many posters and bulletins will not soon be forgotten, especially when created locally.

Certain objects communicate at different seasons such as an advent wreath, a lenten veil, palm branches, and a paschal candle. Symbols pertain to different occasions too: a star, a crown of thorns, tongues of flame, and so on. The absence of things is also a powerful form of communication. The absence of any flowers and candles during Holy Week can say much.

A word of caution is necessary. These colors, textures, images, or objects are not decoration or ornaments. If they are used as such, they are trivialities not worth the time or effort they consume. But if used to add one more dimension to our perception of the good news, they can well be worth considerable effort and expense. Much work goes into a sermon, meant to be preached only once. Much work from a broader segment of the community can well go into visual forms of presenting the gospel, even though these forms, like the sermon, may be disposable art forms. Some ideas are suggested on the pages that follow.

All in all, we are called to proclaim the gospel of salvation by every means we can. The church's year of grace and the lectionary based on it are two vital resources in doing this. If keeping time with the church can make better Christians of us, it is well worth exploring all the possibilities such discipline can offer. It is hoped that the resources that follow will provide some help in that direction.

NOTES

1. *Early Christian Fathers*, Cyril Richardson, ed. (Philadelphia: The Westminster, Press, 1953), p. 96.
2. *The Apostolic Fathers*, Kirsopp Lake, trans. (Cambridge: Harvard University Press), 1965, I, 331.
3. *Documents of the Christian Church*, Henry Bettenson, ed. (New York: Oxford University Press), 1952, p. 6.
4. Richardson, *Early Christian Fathers*, p. 287.
5. Kirsopp Lake, *Apostolic Fathers*, I, 397.
6. Bettenson, *Documents*, p. 27.
7. Richardson, *Early Christian Fathers*, p. 174.
8. James Donaldson, ed., *Ante-Nicene Fathers* (hereafter *ANF*; New York: Charles Scribners, 1899), Vol. 7, 469.
9. *Baptismal Instructions*, Paul W. Harkins, trans. Ancient Christian Writers (Westminster, Md.: Newman, 1963), Vol. 31, p. 127.
10. "On Baptism," S. Thelwall, trans. *ANF*, Vol. 3, p. 678.
11. Eusebius, *The History of the Church*, G. A. Williamson, trans. (Baltimore: Penguin Books, 1965), p. 230.
12. *Egeria's Travels*, John Wilkinson, trans. (London: S.P.C.K., 1971), pp. 132-33.
13. *Letters*, Wilfrid Parsons, trans. Fathers of the Church (New York: Fathers of the Church, 1951), Vol. 12, 283.
14. *Cyril of Jerusalem and Nemesius of Emesa*, William Telfer, trans. (Philadelphia: The Westminster Press, 1955), p. 68.
15. Parsons, *Letters*, Vol. 12, pp. 284-85.
16. "On Baptism," *ANF*, Vol. 3, p. 678.
17. "Life of Constantine the Great," E. C. Richardson, trans., *Nicene and Post-Nicene Fathers*, Second Series, (New York: Christian Literature Co., 1890), Vol. 1, p. 557.
18. John Chrysostom, *Opera Omnia*, Bernard de Montfaucon, ed. (Paris: Gaume, 1834), Vol. 2, p. 418.
19. *Ibid.*, p. 436.
20. Cited by L. Duchesne, *Christian Worship*, 5th ed. (London: S.P.C.K., 1923), p. 260, n. 3.
21. "De Corona," *ANF*, Vol. 3, p. 94.

22. Chrysostom, *Opera Omnia*, Vol. 1, p. 608.
23. "Formula Missae," Bard Thompson, *Liturgies of the Western Church* (Cleveland: Meridian Books, 1961), p. 109.
24. "Book of Discipline," *John Knox's History of the Reformation in Scotland* (London: Thomas Nelson and Sons, 1949), Vol. 2, p. 281.
25. "The Sunday Service," Thompson, *Liturgies*, p. 417.
26. *The Christian Year: A Suggestive Guide for the Worship of the Church*, drafted and revised by Fred Winslow Adams (New York: Committee on Worship, Federal Council of the Churches of Christ in America), 2nd ed. (rev.), 1940, p. 9.
27. *The Christian Year and Lectionary Reform*, (London: SCM Press, 1958).
28. *The Church's Year of Grace*, 5 vols., (Collegeville, Minn.: Liturgical Press, 1964-5).
29. (Nashville: Abingdon, 1976).
30. (Nashville: Abingdon, 1970).

—III—

RESOURCES FOR
THE SEASONS, SUNDAYS,
AND SPECIAL DAYS

On the following pages opening prayers, lections, psalms, hymns, and visuals are suggested for each of the seasons, Sundays, and special days as listed in the calendar in chapter 1. The calendar, lectionary, and psalms are the same as those given on pages 48-57 of *Word and Table: A Basic Pattern of Sunday Worship for United Methodists* (SWR 3), with the following changes:

Several changes have been made in the names of seasons and days. The term "Easter Season" is used instead of "Season of Easter," since it is simpler and makes clear the parallel between it and the Christmas Season. The term "Season after the Epiphany" is used instead of "Epiphany Season" to be consistent with the use of the term "Season after Pentecost" and to clarify the fact that the Epiphany closes the Christmas Season in much the same way that the Day of Pentecost closes the Easter Season. Easter Eve, or Easter Vigil, may also be called the First Service of Easter to indicate that it may be celebrated early Easter Day and to hold it up as being the oldest and theologically most important celebration of Easter, and indeed of the whole calendar. The later service on Easter Day or the Resurrection of the Lord may accordingly be called the Second Service of Easter. The last Sunday after Pentecost may be called Christ the King.

The lectionary has been adjusted on the Sundays after Pentecost. While the Sundays after Pentecost continue to be called "__th Sunday after Pentecost" in our calendar, the lections are determined not by what Sunday it is after Pentecost but by the date in the civil year. On Sunday, October 8, for example, the set of lections numbered 59 is used, since they are intended for the Sunday that falls between October 2 and 8 inclusive; but that Sunday would still be announced as a particular Sunday *whatever Sunday it is* after Pentecost. This system follows the new *Book of Common Prayer* and means that on any given Sunday after Pentecost our lections will coincide with those of the Episcopal and Roman Catholic churches rather than being one or more Sundays out of phase with them, as can happen with our lectionary as published in *Word and Table*. Note, however, that in keeping with ecumenical usage the lections for Trinity Sunday are always used on the First Sunday after Pentecost, regardless of the date.

Finally, a number of revisions has been made in the lectionary itself so that it corresponds more closely with the other denominational versions. These revisions were needed because there have been extensive changes in the Episcopal and Lutheran versions of the lectionary since the version of the lectionary published in *Word and Table* was first prepared by the Consultation on Church Union. The same consensus principles set forth on pages 65-66 of *Word and Table* have been reapplied, and the result is the revised lectionary which follows. In this revision alternative lections are provided in a number of cases where the other denominational versions give two different lections, neither of which is provided for elsewhere in our lectionary. The lection given first is preferred, but circumstances may sometimes make the alternative more fitting. One of the consensus principles has been to give the most inclusive version of each lection—that is, to begin with the earliest verse at which any version begins and continue through the last verse included in any version. For this reason the lections are sometimes long, and it is important to emphasize that they can always be shortened.

Before approving these revisions at its October 1977 meeting, the Section on Worship discussed them with the Worship Commission of the Consultation on Church Union at the commission's meeting earlier the same month. The commission indicated that it had no desire to inhibit these revisions. Later, at its April 1979 meeting, the commission voted to adopt these same revisions for The Consultation on Church Union.

Readers wishing futher information about the lectionary are referred to *Word and Table* (Abingdon, 1976) and are invited to write the Section on Worship, PO Box 840, Nashville, Tennessee 37202 for a listing of preaching, worship, musical, and study resources based on the lectionary.

The calendar and lectionary are in a process of development, and the many denominations involved are working together to improve them and to bring the denominational versions into even closer harmony with one another. Ministers and congregations are invited to send suggestions to the Section on Worship at the above address.

Notes on the Hymn Suggestions

Hymn numbers refer to *The Book of Hymns* (*The Methodist Hymnal*, 1966). A number of selections from other hymnals and songbooks are also listed, in the attempt to make available a variety of hymnic resources of more recent composition. These supplemental listings are indicated by code letters preceding the actual number of the hymn in the book. For example, *EP* 61 refers to Number 61 in *Ecumenical Praise*. Full titles of these hymnals, together with their denominational affiliation or other publication data and the code letters as used in this book, are listed below. If you do not have these other denominational hymnals, neighboring pastors or musicians of the respective denominations may be willing to lend you single copies for reference, or direct you to their denominational publishing houses. Some of the hymnals may also be found in neighboring college libraries.

The tunes given with the various hymns, both in *The Book of Hymns* and the other hymnals, generally speaking, are worthy tunes and appropriate to the texts. We urge their use wherever possible. However, in some situations an unfamiliar tune will be a stumbling block to effective use of the hymn in the congregation. In such instances we urge you to find and use another more familiar tune that fits the text. Use the metrical index in the back of the hymnal. Study the words and the prospective tunes carefully to be sure that the accents of the words fit the accents of the tune and also that the mood of the tune is appropriate to the words.

Not all the hymns will be suitable for congregational singing, at least at first, especially the less familiar and some of the supplemental hymns. These may be offered by choirs or soloists, sometimes with the congregation joining on a refrain or on the last stanza.

The first hymn in each list, usually, is intended to catch up the thread or theme that runs through all the lessons for that particular day, if this is possible. Other hymns in the list may reach a bit further afield, or may relate specifically to one of the lections. Sometimes a hymn will make an especially apt transition from one lection to the next. Occasionally the successive stanzas of a hymn will amplify the successive passages of one or more lections, and can be interspersed through the readings. An obvious example is Hymn 362 and the Old Testament and Gospel readings for the Second Sunday in Advent, Year B.

As you plan for worship and preaching for the several Sundays of a season, be alert to themes that may run through the lessons for two or more Sundays in succession. Sometimes a hymn listed for one Sunday may be equally appropriate on neighboring Sundays. Repeated use of such a hymn will also help the congregation to learn it better.

No attempt is made here to meet other hymnic needs in the service, such as opening hymns. These will be suggested by the seasons and by the concerns of general praise, invocation, and affirmation.

Identification of Hymnals

BNC   *Break Not the Circle*, words by Fred Kaan, music by Doreen Potter. Hope Publishing Company, Carol Stream, Illinois 60187. Some of these texts are given other tunes by Ron Klusmeier in *Worship the Lord*, published by Frederick Harris Music Company, 529 Speers Road, Oakville, Ontario, Canada L6K 2G4.

C   *The Hymn Book* (1970), published jointly by the United Church of Canada and the Anglican Church of Canada. United Church Publishing House, 47 Coldwater Road, Don Mills, Ontario, Canada M3B 1Y9.

CH   *The Covenant Hymnal* (1973), of the Evangelical Covenant Church.

EP   *Ecumenical Praise* (1977), supplemental hymnal compiled by Carlton Young and others, Hope Publishing Company, Carol Stream, Illinois 60187.

EUB   *The Hymnal* (1957), of the former Evangelical United Brethren Church.

HFL   *Hymns of Faith and Life* (1976), of the Free Methodist Church and the Wesleyan Church.

MHSS   *More Hymns and Spiritual Songs* (1971; new enlarged edition published 1977), an Episcopal hymnal supplement. Walton Music Corporation, 17 West 60th Street, New York, New York 10023.

OHT   *100 Hymns for Today* (1969), published by William Clowes and Son for the Proprietors of *Hymns Ancient and Modern* (England), available in the United States through Morehouse-Barlow, 14 East 41st Street, New York, New York 10017.

SB   *Baptist Hymnal* (1975) of the Southern Baptist Convention.

SS   *Songs and Hymns from Sweden* (1976), translated into English by Fred Kaan, published in

England by Stainer and Bell, distributed in the United States by Galaxy Music Corporation, 2121 Broadway, New York, New York 10023.

UCC   *The Hymnal* (1974) of the United Church of Christ (former Congregational churches and the former Evangelical and Reformed Church).

WB   *The Worshipbook* (1972), of the Presbyterian churches (UPCUSA, PCUS, and Cumberland).

WP   *Westminster Praise* (1976), supplemental hymnal compiled by Erik Routley. Hinshaw Music, PO Box 470, Chapel Hill, North Carolina 27514.

ADVENT SEASON

1. Opening prayer for use in Advent

> God of Israel,
>> with expectant hearts
>> we your people await Christ's coming.
>
> As once he came in humility,
>> so now may he come in glory,
>> that he may make all things perfect
>> in your everlasting kingdom.
>
> For he is Lord for ever and ever. **Amen.**

2. Advent antiphons

> O Wisdom proceeding from the mouth of the highest,
> reaching from eternity to eternity
> and disposing all things with strength and sweetness:
>> **Come, teach us the way of knowledge.**
>
> O Lord and Leader of Israel,
> you appeared to Moses in the burning bush
> and delivered the law to him on Sinai:
>> **Come redeem us by your outstretched arm.**
>
> O Root of Jesse,
> you stand as a sign of the people;
> before you rulers do not open their mouths;
> to you the nations shall pray:
>> **Come and deliver us, do not delay.**
>
> O Key of David and Scepter of Israel,
> you open and no one shuts;
> you shut and no one opens:
>> **Come and release from prison those who sit in darkness and in the shadow of death.**
>
> O Dayspring, splendor of eternal light and sun of
> righteousness:
>> **Come and enlighten those who sit in darkness and in the shadow of death.**
>
> O King of nations,
> their desire and the cornerstone that binds them in
> one:

Come and save those whom you formed of clay.
O Emmanuel, our King and lawgiver,
the expectation and Savior of the nations:
Come and save us, O Lord our God.

The Book of Worship, 1964, altered

3. Visuals

Purple, blue or gray, or somber hues; rough or coarse textures. The custom of using an advent wreath with four candles (traditionally suspended so as to suggest the shape of a tree) is a good way to strengthen the sense of anticipation. The color of the candles is not important, though for United Methodist use they should all be the same. One more candle is lighted on each successive Sunday in Advent until all four are lighted on the Fourth Sunday in Advent. Occasionally a fifth candle—a white Christ Candle—is lighted on Christmas.

The names of Jesus in the above advent antiphons may suggest visual possibilities for banners, bulletins, and so on. Appropriate visual symbols for Advent include a plumb line (Amos), trumpets, scales of justice, the root or tree of Jesse, and the words "Emmanuel," "Maranatha," and "Come, Lord Jesus."

1. FIRST SUNDAY IN ADVENT

(Sunday between November 27 and December 3 inclusive)

Year A (1980, 1983, 1986)

Isaiah 2:1-5; Romans 13:8-14; Matthew 24:36-44
Psalm 122 or *Book of Hymns* 562
Hymns: 477, 283, 363, 353 (Romans), "God of Truth, from Everlasting"[1]

Year B (1981, 1984, 1987)

Isaiah 63:16–64:9*a*; I Corinthians 1:1-9; Mark 13:24-37
Psalm 80:1-7 or *Book of Hymns* 562
Hymns: 358, 78, 154 (Isaiah), 356 (Isaiah), 353 (I Cor.)

Year C (1979, 1982, 1985)

Jeremiah 33:14-16; I Thessalonians 3:9–4:2; Luke 21:25-36
Psalm 25:1-10 or *Book of Hymns* 562
Hymns: 364, 354 (I Thess.), 545, *UCC* 64

2. SECOND SUNDAY IN ADVENT

(Sunday between December 4 and 10 inclusive)

Year A (1980, 1983, 1986)

Isaiah 11:1-10; Romans 15:4-13; Matthew 3:1-12
Psalm 72:1-19 or *Book of Hymns* 597
Hymns: 78, 356, 362, *EUB* 75, *MHSS* 57

Year B (1981, 1984, 1987)

Isaiah 40:1-11; II Peter 3:8-15*a*, 18; Mark 1:1-8
Psalm 85 or *Book of Hymns* 597
Hymns: 362, 354, 364 (II Peter), 468 (II Peter)

Year C (1979, 1982, 1985)

Malachi 3:1-4 or Baruch 5:1-9; Philippians 1:1-11; Luke 3:1-6
Psalm 126 or *Book of Hymns* 597
Hymns: 362 (Luke), 359, 355 (Malachi), 353, *SS* 20 (Malachi/Philippians), 78

3. THIRD SUNDAY IN ADVENT
(Sunday between December 11 and 17 inclusive)

Year A (1980, 1983, 1986)

Isaiah 35:1-10; James 5:7-10; Matthew 11:2-11
Psalm 146 or *Book of Hymns* 612
Hymns: 359, 356, *BNC* 2

Year B (1981, 1984, 1987)

Isaiah 61:1-4, 8-11; I Thessalonians 5:12-28; John 1:6-8, 19-28
Luke 1:46b-55 or *Book of Hymns* 612
Hymns: 359, 283, 363, 101 (I Thess.), *EUB* 75, *BNC* 2

Year C (1979, 1982, 1985)

Zephaniah 3:14-20; Philippians 4:4-9; Luke 3:7-18
Isaiah 12:2-6 or *Book of Hymns* 612
Hymns: 360, 359, 353, 483 (Philippians)

4. FOURTH SUNDAY IN ADVENT
(Sunday between December 18 and 24 inclusive)

Year A (1980, 1983, 1986)

Isaiah 7:10-17; Romans 1:1-7; Matthew 1:18-25
Psalm 24 or *Book of Hymns* 561
Hymns: 381, *MHSS* 62, 385, *EP* 61

Year B (1981, 1984, 1987)

II Samuel 7:1-16; Romans 16:25-27; Luke 1:26-38
Psalm 89:1-4, 14-18 or *Book of Hymns* 561
Hymns: 360, 78, 283, 123 (II Samuel), 324 (Luke)

Year C (1979, 1982, 1985)

Micah 5:1-4; Hebrews 10:5-10; Luke 1:39-55
Psalm 80:1-7 or *Book of Hymns* 561
Hymns: 355, 362, 378, 381, 389 (Hebrews), *MHSS* 62

CHRISTMAS SEASON

1. Opening prayer for use in the Christmas Season

> O Christ,
> your wonderful birth is meaningless
>   unless we are born again.
> Your death is meaningless
>   unless we die to sin.
> Your resurrection is meaningless
>   if you only have been raised.
> Bring us now to such love for you
>   that we may enjoy you forever.
> For all things in the heavens and on earth
>   are yours eternally. **Amen.**
>
>> Dean Eric Milner-White,
>> *A Cambridge Bede Book* altered

2. Opening prayer for use in the Christmas Season

> God, creator of all life
>   you made us in your image
>   and sent your Son to be our flesh.
> Grant us now in this glad time of his birth,
>   that we, who have been born again through his
>   grace, may daily find all things made new in him.
> For he lives and reigns with you and the
>   Holy Spirit. **Amen.**

3. Visuals

> White, yellow, gold, or the finest and most joyful available, fine and elegant textures.
>
> The use of a Christmas crèche (Nativity, Praesepio) from Christmas Eve up to the Presentation (February 2) may be a useful ministry to both children and adults. Appropriate visual symbols for the Christmas Season include a manger, angels, and shepherds. Key words such as "Peace on Earth," "Gloria in Excelsis," may be used to suggest visual possibilities.

5. CHRISTMAS OR THE NATIVITY OF JESUS CHRIST
(Christmas Eve and Christmas Day)

Year A (1980, 1983, 1986)

Isaiah 9:1-7; Titus 2:11-15; Luke 2:1-20
Psalm 96 or *Book of Hymns* 585
Hymns: 374, 394 (Luke), 361 (Isaiah), *UCC* 103

Year B (1981, 1984, 1987)

Isaiah 62:6-12; Titus 3:4-7; Luke 2:1-20
Psalm 98 or *Book of Hymns* 585
Hymns: 388/387, 394 (Luke), 374, 359 (Isaiah)

Year C (1979, 1982, 1985)

Isaiah 52:6-10; Hebrews 1:1-12; John 1:1-18
Psalm 97 or *Book of Hymns* 585
Hymns: 357 (John), 388/387, 385, 390 (Isaiah)

6. FIRST SUNDAY AFTER CHRISTMAS

(Sunday between December 26 and January 1 inclusive)
May be celebrated on December 25 when it falls on a
Sunday and the Christmas lections have been used on
Christmas Eve.

Year A (1980/81, 1983/84, 1986/87)

Isaiah 63:7-9 or Ecclesiastes 3:1-9, 14-17; Galatians 4:4-7;
John 1:1-18
Psalm 111 or Book of Hymns 590
Hymns: 392, 391, 469 (John), WB 598 (John), 509
(Ecclesiastes), 510 (Ecclesiastes), MHSS 62

Year B (1981/82, 1984/85, 1987/88)

Isaiah 45:22-25 or Ecclesiasticus 3:2-6, 12-14; Colossians
3:12-21; Luke 2:22-40
Psalm 111 or Book of Hymns 590
Hymns: 391, 392, 389, 390, 80, 355 (Colossians), 74
(Colossians), 385 (Luke)

Year C (1979/80, 1982/83, 1985/86)

Jeremiah 31:10-13 or Ecclesiasticus 3:2-6, 12-14; Hebrews
2:10-18; Luke 2:41-52
Psalm 111 or Book of Hymns 590
Hymns: 388/387 (Jeremiah/Hebrews), 389 (Hebrews), 80
(Luke), 391

7. SECOND SUNDAY AFTER CHRISTMAS

(Sunday between January 2 and 5 inclusive)
May be celebrated on January 1 if the lections for the First
Sunday after Christmas have been used on December 25.
May be replaced by Epiphany Sunday.

Year A (1981, 1984, 1987)

Isaiah 61:10–62:3 or Ecclesiasticus 24:1-2, 8-12; Ephesians
 1:3-6, 15-23; Matthew 2:13-15, 19-23
Psalm 147:12-20 or *Book of Hymns* 580
Hymns: 398, 90, 483 (Ephesians), 75, 80, *EP* 28, *UCC* 103

Year B (1979, 1982, 1985)

Jeremiah 31:7-14 or Ecclesiasticus 24:1-2, 8-12; Revelation
 21:22–22:2; John 1:1-18
Psalm 147:12-20 or *Book of Hymns* 580
Hymns: 398, 469 (John), 481 (Revelation), 401, 357 (John),
 WB 598 (John)

Year C (1980, 1983, 1986)

Isaiah 61:10–62:3 or Ecclesiasticus 24:1-2, 8-12; I Corinth-
 ians 1:18-25; Matthew 2:13-15, 19-23
Psalm 147:12-20 or *Book of Hymns* 580
Hymns: 398, 84 (I Corinthians/Matthew), 75, 256
(Matthew)

8. THE EPIPHANY OR
THE MANIFESTATION OF GOD IN JESUS CHRIST
(January 6)
May be celebrated the first Sunday in January.

Years A, B, and C

Isaiah 60:1-6; Ephesians 3:1-12; Matthew 2:1-12
Psalm 72:1-19 or *Book of Hymns* 577
Hymns: 397, 398, 400, 405, EP 28
Opening prayer

> God of all glory,
>> by the guidance of a star
>> you led the Wise Men to worship the Christ Child.
> By the light of faith
>> lead us to your glory in heaven.
> We ask this through Christ our Lord. **Amen.**
>> Altered from *The Roman Sacramentary*, hereafter *Sac.*

Visuals

White, yellow, gold, or the finest and most joyful available, fine and elegant textures.

Images of the Wise Men or their gifts—gold, frankincense (which may be burnt as incense), and myrrh—are appropriate. The Wise Men traditionally represent the three races of humanity. This can be suggested by the choice of colors for faces and hands. Three crowns also symbolize the Wise Men. "The first of the signs by which Jesus revealed his glory" (John 2:11) was the wedding feast at Cana. This can be indicated by one or six water jars.

SEASON AFTER THE EPIPHANY

1. Opening prayer for use in the Season after the Epiphany

Lord Jesus Christ,
from the moment of your birth
   God was manifest to us.
By your mighty signs and life-giving teachings
   you revealed your glory
   and made the Father known to us.
Reveal to us the heart of God
   that our hearts may be dazzled by its brightness.
For all things come through you, Lord. **Amen.**

2. Visuals

   Green, except that white is used on the First and Last Sundays after the Epiphany (the Baptism of the Lord and the Transfiguration of the Lord).

   Throughout the Season after the Epiphany visual materials may witness to the mighty signs and teachings (from the Baptism of the Lord to the Transfiguration) by which God became manifest in the person and work of Jesus Christ. The Gospel lections for this season suggest weekly visual possibilities.

9. FIRST SUNDAY AFTER
THE EPIPHANY OR THE BAPTISM OF THE LORD

(Sunday between January 7 and 13 inclusive)
If Sunday falls on January 7, it is suggested that the Epiphany and the Baptism of the Lord be celebrated together.

Year A (1981, 1984, 1987)

Isaiah 42:1-9; Acts 10:34-38; Matthew 3:13-17
Psalm 29:1-4, 9-10 or *Book of Hymns* 583
Hymns: 398, 359, *MHSS* 62, 476

Year B (1979, 1982, 1985)

Isaiah 42:1-9; Acts 10:34-38; Mark 1:4-11
Psalm 29:1-4, 9-10 or *Book of Hymns* 583
Hymns 398, 407, 359, *UCC* 75

Year C (1980, 1983, 1986)

Isaiah 42:1-9; Acts 10:34-38; Luke 3:15-17, 21-22
Psalm 29:1-4, 9-10 or *Book of Hymns* 583
Hymns: 359, 398, 410, *WB* 598
Opening prayer

> Living God,
> > when the Spirit descended on Jesus
> > at his baptism in Jordan's water
> > you revealed him as your own beloved Son.
> Keep us, your children
> > who have been born of water and the Spirit,
> > always faithful to him
> > who is Lord for ever and ever. **Amen.**
> > > > *Sac.* altered

Visuals

White. Symbols of baptism, especially water itself, are appropriate for this Sunday. The baptismal shell (a scallop), a descending dove, and a cross standing in water are other possibilities.

10. SECOND SUNDAY AFTER THE EPIPHANY
(Sunday between January 14 and 20 inclusive)

Year A (1981, 1984, 1987)

Isaiah 49:1-7; I Corinthians 1:1-9; John 1:29-41
Psalm 40:1-11 or *Book of Hymns* 568
Hymns: 401, *WB* 598, 253, 329, 85, 341 *(John)*

Year B (1979, 1982, 1985)

1 Samuel 3:1-20; I Corinthians 6:11b-20; John 1:35-51
Psalm 67 or *Book of Hymns* 568
Hymns: 107, 75, 133 (I Corinthians), 84 (I Corinthians), 274
(I Samuel), 85

Year C (1980, 1983, 1986)

Isaiah 62:1-5; I Corinthians 12:1-11; John 2:1-12
Psalm 36:5-10 or *Book of Hymns* 568
Hymns: 301, 530, *SB* 259, 233 (Isaiah/I Corinthians), 257 (I
Corinthians/John), *HFL* 491[2], *BNC* 2

11. THIRD SUNDAY AFTER THE EPIPHANY
(Sunday between January 21 and 27 inclusive)

Year A (1981, 1984, 1987)

Isaiah 9:1-4 or Amos 3:1-8; I Corinthians 1:10-17; Matthew
4:12-23
Psalm 27:1, 4, 13-14 or *Book of Hymns* 563
Hymns: 107, "Lord of Life That Came to Flower,"[3] 407, 398
(Isaiah), 152, 408

Year B (1979, 1982, 1985)

Jonah 3:1-5, 10; I Corinthians 7:29-35; Mark 1:14-20
Psalm 62:5-12 or *Book of Hymns* 563
Hymns: 406, 107, 152, 177

Year C (1980, 1983, 1986)

Nehemiah 8:1-4a, 5-6, 8-10; I Corinthians 12:12-30; Luke
1:1-4; 4:14-21
Psalm 113 or *Book of Hymns* 563
Hymns: 299, 193 (I Corinthians), 407, *WB* 619 (I Corinthians), 408

12. FOURTH SUNDAY AFTER THE EPIPHANY

(Sunday between January 28 and February 3 inclusive)
If this is the Last Sunday after the Epiphany, use 17.

Year A (1981, 1984, 1987)

Micah 6:1-8 or Zephaniah 2:3; 3:11-13; I Corinthians 1:18-31; Matthew 5:1-12
Psalm 1 or Book of Hymns 554
Hymns: 276, SB 103, 90, 282, 266, 52

Year B (1979, 1982, 1985)

Deuteronomy 18:15-22; I Corinthians 8:1-13; Mark 1:21-28
Psalm 1 or Book of Hymns 554
Hymns: 81, 341, 409, 156 (I Corinthians), 164, 75, 87, 90

Year C (1980, 1983, 1986)

Jeremiah 1:4-10, 17-19; I Corinthians 12:27–13:13; Luke 4:21-32
Psalm 71:1-6, 15-17 or Book of Hymns 554
Hymns: 476, SB 410, 80 (Luke), WB 641 (I Corinthians) 202, SB 309, 267

13. FIFTH SUNDAY AFTER THE EPIPHANY

(Sunday between February 4 and 10 inclusive)
If this is the Last Sunday after the Epiphany, use 17.

Year A (1981, 1984, 1987)

Isaiah 58:5-10; I Corinthians 2:1-11; Matthew 5:13-20
Psalm 112:4-9 or Book of Hymns 599
Hymns: 407, 329, 202, "Lord of Life That Came to Flower,"[3] EP 66, CH 552[4]

Year B (1979, 1982, 1985)

Job 7:1-7; I Corinthians 9:16-23; Mark 1:29-39
Psalm 147:1-12 or Book of Hymns 599
Hymns: CH 552,[4] 204, 501 (Mark), 479, 212 (Job), 161 (Job), 170

Year C (1980, 1983, 1986)

Isaiah 6:1-13; I Corinthians 15:1-11 or I Cor. 14:12b-20; Luke 5:1-11
Psalm 138 or Book of Hymns 599
Hymns: 107, 200 (Isaiah/Luke), 408, 277 (I Corinthians 14)

14. SIXTH SUNDAY AFTER THE EPIPHANY

(Sunday between February 11 and 17 inclusive)
If this is the Last Sunday after the Epiphany, use 17.

Year A (1981, 1984, 1987)

Deuteronomy 30:15-20 or Ecclesiasticus 15:15-20; I Corinthians 2:6-13; Matthew 5:20-37

Psalm 119:1-16 or *Book of Hymns* 564

Hymns: 403, 195, "We Want to Know, Lord, Touch Our Minds,"[5] 256, 254, "God of Truth, from Everlasting"[1]

Year B (1979, 1982, 1985)

II Kings 5:1-15b or Leviticus 13:1-2, 44-46; I Corinthians 9:24-27; 10:31—11:1; Mark 1:40-45

Psalm 32 or *Book of Hymns* 564

Hymns: 407, 158/157, 276 (I Corinthians), 279/280 (I Corinthians), 411

Year C (1980, 1983, 1986)

Jeremiah 17:5-10; I Corinthians 15:12-20; Luke 6:17-26

Psalm 1 or *Book of Hymns* 564

Hymns: SB 201[6], 276, 90, 521 (Jeremiah), 341 (I Corinthians) SS 7[7] (Luke)

15. SEVENTH SUNDAY AFTER THE EPIPHANY

(Sunday between February 18 and 24 inclusive)
If this is the Last Sunday after the Epiphany, use 17.

Year A (1981, 1984, 1987)

Leviticus 19:1-2, 9-18; I Corinthians 3:10-11, 16-23; Matthew 5:38-48
Psalm 103:1-13 or *Book of Hymns* 587
Hymns: 199 (Leviticus/Matthew), 48 (I Corinthians), 278, 286, *CH* 555[a] (Leviticus/Matthew), *WP* 51 (I Corinthians)

Year B (1979, 1982, 1985)

Isaiah 43:15-25; II Corinthians 1:18-22; Mark 2:1-12
Psalm 41 or *Book of Hymns* 587
Hymns: 178, 299, 284, 281 (Isaiah/II Corinthians), 283 (II Corinthians) 224 (II Corinthians), 227 (II Corinthians), 125/126 (II Corinthians/Mark)

Year C (1980, 1983, 1986)

Genesis 45:3-11, 21-28; I Corinthians 15:35-38a, 42-50; Luke 6:27-38
Psalm 37:3-10 or *Book of Hymns* 587
Hymns: *SB* 309, 278, 408, 199, 188

16. EIGHTH SUNDAY AFTER THE EPIPHANY

(Sunday between February 25 and 29 inclusive)
If this is the Last Sunday after the Epiphany, use 17. May also be used on the Sunday between May 24 and 28 inclusive, if it is the Second Sunday after Pentecost.

Year A (1981, 1984, 1987)

Isaiah 49:8-18; I Corinthians 4:1-13; Matthew 6:24-34
Psalm 62 or *Book of Hymns* 573
Hymns: SS 7[7], 196, 256, 231 (Matthew), "The Earth Is the Lord's,"[9] 182, 186

Year B (1979, 1982, 1985)

Hosea 2:14-23; II Corinthians 3:1b-6; Mark 2:18-22
Psalm 103:1-13 or *Book of Hymns* 573
Hymns: 476, 188, 409, 410, 528

Year C (1980, 1983, 1986)

Jeremiah 7:1-15 or Ecclesiasticus 27:4-7; I Corinthians 15:50-58; Luke 6:39-49
Psalm 92 or *Book of Hymns* 573
Hymns: 278, 254, 440 (I Corinthians), 475 (Jeremiah), 484 (Jeremiah) 222

17. LAST SUNDAY AFTER THE EPIPHANY
OR THE TRANSFIGURATION OF THE LORD

Occurs regardless of how many Sundays there are after the Epiphany.

Year A (1981, 1984, 1987)

Exodus 24:12-18; II Peter 1:16-21; Matthew 17:1-9
Psalm 2:6-11 or *Book of Hymns* 584
Hymns: 79, 85, *EUB* 93, 153, 152, "God of Truth, from Everlasting,"[1] *MHSS* 74

Year B (1979, 1982, 1985)

II Kings 2:1-12a; II Corinthians 3:12–4:2; Mark 9:2-9
Psalm 50:1-6 or *Book of Hymns* 584
Hymns: 479, 398, 409, 178, *MHSS* 74

Year C (1980, 1983, 1986)

Deuteronomy 34:1-12; II Corinthians 4:3-6; Luke 9:28-36
Psalm 99:1-5 or *Book of Hymns* 584
Hymns: 479, 398, 202, 549, *MHSS* 74
Opening prayer

> God our Father and Mother,
> before his death in shame
> > your Son went to the mountaintop
> > and you revealed his life in glory.
> Where prophets witnessed to him,
> > you proclaimed him your Son,
> > but he returned to die among us.
> Help us face evil with courage,
> > knowing that all things, even death,
> > are subject to your transformation.
> We ask this through Christ our Lord. **Amen.**

Or, opening prayer for Season after the Epiphany.

Visuals
> White. The visuals could suggest Christ in a blaze of glory, especially with shining garments.

LENT

1. Opening prayer for use in Lent

> Creator God,
> in this our time of repentance
> we call out for your mercy.
> Turn us back to you
> and to the new life Christ restored
> by his perfect obedience even to death on a cross.
> For he lives and reigns as our Redeemer for ever and
> ever. **Amen.**
>
> *Sac.* altered

2. Visuals

Purple, blue, gray, dark earth colors, or any somber hues; rough coarse textures.

Some churches use a lenten veil to cover the cross in the church and/or statues and paintings. The veil may be made from mesh or cheesecloth dyed a purple or blue or gray. It covers the cross or images completely and may be gathered at the bottom. Because of the transparent nature of the veil, the cross remains visible yet shrouded. Some confine this to Holy Week, but it may be better to have the veil used throughout Lent unless there are daily services. If weddings are not discouraged during this period, it may be well to make it easy to remove the lenten veil on such occasions. Lent focuses our attention on the cross, and the lenten veil, though it partly conceals the cross, also calls attention to it. Symbols of the Passion—crown of thorns, whip, ladder, headboard, sponge, spear, nails, crowing cock, bag of coins—may be used, especially during Holy Week.

18. ASH WEDNESDAY
(seventh Wednesday before Easter)

Year A (1981, 1984, 1987)

Joel 2:12-19; II Corinthians 5:20b–6:10; Matthew 6:1-6, 16-21
Psalm 51:1-17 or *Book of Hymns* 571
Hymns: 94, 103, 95, 261

Year B (1979, 1982, 1985)

Isaiah 58:1-12; James 1:12-18; Mark 2:15-20
Psalm 51:1-17 or *Book of Hymns* 571
Hymns: 102, 94, 103, *MHSS* 37

Year C (1980, 1983, 1986)

Zechariah 7:4-10; I Corinthians 9:19-27; Luke 5:29-35
Psalm 51:1-17 or *Book of Hymns* 571
Hymns: 102, 413, 173, 112 (Luke), 129 (Luke), EP 114
Opening Prayer

Most holy God,
your Son came to serve sinners.
We come to this season of repentance,
    confessing our sinfulness,
    asking for new and honest hearts,
    and the healing power of your forgiveness.
Grant this through Christ our Lord. **Amen.**
Sac. altered and *Contemporary Worship 6*
(hereafter *CW6*) altered

Or, opening prayer for Lent above.

19. FIRST SUNDAY IN LENT

Year A (1981, 1984, 1987)

Genesis 2:4b-9, 15-17, 25; 3:1-7; Romans 5:12-21; Matthew
4:1-11
Psalm 130 or *Book of Hymns* 581
Hymns: 112, 167, 78 (Genesis), 114, 94, WP 27

Year B (1979, 1982, 1985)

Genesis 9:8-17; I Peter 3:18-22; Mark 1:9-15
Psalm 25:3-9 or *Book of Hymns* 581
Hymns: 112, 237, 104, 120 (I Peter), CH 357

Year C (1980, 1983, 1986)

Deuteronomy 26:1-11; Romans 10:5-13; Luke 4:1-13
Psalm 91 or *Book of Hymns* 581
Hymns: 103, 271, 95, 113, UCC 226[10]

20. SECOND SUNDAY IN LENT

Year A (1981, 1984, 1987)

Genesis 12:1-8; Romans 4:1-17; John 3:1-17
Psalm 33:12-22 or *Book of Hymns* 569
Hymns: 103, 141, 137 (Romans), 47, 48, 257

Year B (1979, 1982, 1985)

Genesis 22:1-18 or Genesis 28:10-22; Romans 8:31-39;
Mark 8:31-38
Psalm: 115:1, 9-18 or *Book of Hymns* 569
Hymns: 413, 173, 170, 52 (Genesis/Romans), 205 (Romans),
222 (Romans), BNC 4 (Romans)

Year C (1980, 1983, 1986)

Genesis 15:1-12, 17-18; Philippians 3:17–4:1; Luke 13:22-
35
Psalm 27:7-14 or *Book of Hymns* 569
Hymns: 112, 205 (Genesis/Philippians), 94 (Luke), 227
(Philippians), 224 (Philippians)

21. THIRD SUNDAY IN LENT

Year A (1981, 1984, 1987)

Exodus 17:3-7; Romans 5:1-11; John 4:5-42
Psalm 95:1-2, 6-11 or *Book of Hymns* 558
Hymns: 205, 152, 339, 341, 118, 293

Year B (1979, 1982, 1985)

Exodus 20:1-17; I Corinthians 1:22-25; John 2:13-25
Psalm 19:7-14 or *Book of Hymns* 558
Hymns: 124, 123, 259, 482, 471, *BNC* 16

Year C (1980, 1983, 1986)

Exodus 3:1-15; I Corinthians 10:1-13; Luke 13:1-9
Psalm 103:1-11 or *Book of Hymns* 558
Hymns: 140, 119, 98 (Exodus), 54 (Exodus), 87
  (I Corinthians)

22. FOURTH SUNDAY IN LENT

Year A (1981, 1984, 1987)

I Samuel 16:1-13; Ephesians 5:8-14; John 9:1-41
Psalm 23 or *Book of Hymns* 598
Hymns: 92, 401, 137, 114, 257

Year B (1979, 1982, 1985)

II Chronicles 36:14-23; Ephesians 2:1-10; John 3:14-21
Psalm 137:1-6 or *Book of Hymns* 598
Hymns: 412, 415, 122, 414, 115 (Ephesians), 430, *MHSS* 9

Year C (1980, 1983, 1986)

Joshua 5:9-12; II Corinthians 5:16-21; Luke 15:1-3, 11-32
Psalm 34:1-8 or *Book of Hymns* 598
Hymns: 122, 114, 119, 193, 92

23. FIFTH SUNDAY IN LENT

Year A *(1981, 1984, 1987)*

Ezekiel 37:1-14; Romans 8:6-19; John 11:1-53
Psalm 116:1-9 or *Book of Hymns* 615
Hymns: 75, 118 (Romans), 123, 432, 115, 124

Year B *(1979, 1982, 1985)*

Jeremiah 31:31-34; Hebrews 5:7-10; John 12:20-33
Psalm 51:10-16 or *Book of Hymns* 615
Hymns: 420, 432, 418, 355, 441 (John)

Year C *(1980, 1983, 1985)*

Isaiah 43:16-21; Philippians 3:8-14; John 8:1-11
Psalm 28:1-3, 6-9 or *Book of Hymns* 615
Hymns: 115, 101, 83, 87, 418 (Philippians), 251, 122

HOLY WEEK

1. Opening Prayer for use in Holy Week

> Lord Jesus,
> One of us betrayed you,
>   another denied you,
>   and all of us have forsaken you.
> Yet you remained faithful,
>   even to death on a cross.
> Strengthen us to persevere in following you.
> For the final victory belongs to you,
>   Lord Jesus. **Amen.**

2. Visuals

Purple, blue, gray, dark earth colors, or any somber hues; rough coarse textures. A deep hue of red may be used, instead, throughout Holy Week.

See suggestions for Lent above. All crosses and images may be veiled for Holy Week and no flowers used. Symbols of the Passion—crown of thorns, whip, ladder, headboard, sponge, spears, nails, crowing cock, drops of blood, bag of coins—are especially appropriate during Holy Week.

24. PALM/PASSION SUNDAY

Year A (1981, 1984, 1987)

Matthew 21:1-11*; Isaiah 50:4-9a; Philippians 2:5-11; Matthew 26:14–27:66

Psalm 22:1-11 or Book of Hymns 559

Hymns: 424 (opening), 427, 432, 74 (Philippians), 76 (Philippians)

Year B (1979, 1982, 1985)

Mark 11:1-11* or John 12:12-16*; Zechariah 9:9-12; Philippians 2:5-11; Mark 14:1-15:47

Psalm 22:7-8, 16-19, 22-23 or Book of Hymns 559

Hymns: 423 (Mark 11), 425 (John 12), 434 (Mark), 414, 74 (Philippians), 359 (Zechariah), 422, 482

Year C (1980, 1983, 1986)

Luke 19:28-40*; Deuteronomy 32:36-39; Philippians 2:5-11; Luke 22:1–23:56

Psalm 31:1-5, 9-16 or Book of Hymns 559

Hymns: 422, 434, 76 (Philippians), 435, 417

Opening prayer

> God our hope,
> today we joyfully acclaim Jesus our Messiah and King.
> Help us to honor him every day
> so we may enjoy our Savior's rule in the new Jerusalem
> where he reigns with you and the Holy Spirit
> for ever and ever. **Amen.**   Sac. altered

Or, opening prayer for Holy Week, above.

Visuals

> Purple, blue, dark earth colors, or any somber hues; rough coarse textures. A deep hue of red may be used instead.

*These are appropriately read at the beginning of the service.

It will be highly desirable to have palm fronds, olive branches, or green branches of any tree or shrub to decorate the church and for the people to carry in procession at the beginning of the service. They need not be large. The long Gospel lessons for today are passion narratives. It often will work best if parts are read by a narrator, a person representing Christ, and by the congregation. It may work best for the Christ figure to stand on a lower level than the narrator until the time of the crucifixion. Necessary stage business will need to be rehearsed in advance by the chief characters. All crosses and images may be veiled for Holy Week (cf. visuals for Lent) and no flowers used.

25. MONDAY IN HOLY WEEK

Years A, B, and C

Isaiah 42:1-9; Hebrews 9:11-15; John 12:1-11
Psalm 36:5-10 or *Book of Hymns* 572
See under "Holy Week" in *Book of Hymns* Topical Index
 (851)

26. TUESDAY IN HOLY WEEK

Years A, B, and C

Isaiah 49:1-9a; I Corinthians 1:18-31; John 12:37-50
Psalm 71:1-12, 15, 17 or *Book of Hymns* 567
See under "Holy Week" in *Book of Hymns* Topical Index
 (851)

27. WEDNESDAY IN HOLY WEEK

Years A, B, and C

Isaiah 50:4-9; Romans 5:6-11; John 13:21-38
Psalm 70:1-2, 4-5 or *Book of Hymns* 578
See under "Holy Week" in *Book of Hymns* Topical Index
 (851)

28. MAUNDY THURSDAY

Year A (1981, 1984, 1987)

Exodus 12:1-14; I Corinthians 11:17-32; John 13:1-17, 34
Psalm 116:12-19 or *Book of Hymns* 591
Hymns: 319, 320/322/323, 321

Year B (1979, 1982, 1985)

Exodus 24:3-11; I Corinthians 10:16-21; Mark 14:12-26 or
   John 13:1-17, 34
Psalm 116:12-19 or *Book of Hymns* 591
Hymns: 320/322/323, 321, 326/327

Year C (1980, 1983, 1986)

Jeremiah 31:31-34; Hebrews 10:16-39; Luke 22:7-30 or John
   13:1-17, 34
Psalm 116:12-19 or *Book of Hymns* 591
Hymns: 320/322/323, 328, 314, 306
Opening prayer at communion

God of love,
we are gathered here to share in the supper
   which your only Son left to his church
   on the night before he died.
He commanded us to celebrate it
   so that we might make his sacrifice our own,
   until we feast anew with him in your kingdom.
We ask this in the name of Jesus the Lord. **Amen.**

Sac. altered

Or, opening prayer for Lent above.

Or, opening prayer for Holy Week above.

Visuals

   The color at the beginning of the evening service can
be purple, or blue, or gray. White or a deep hue of red are
alternative uses. At the end of the service the church may
be stripped of altar cloths, pulpit and lectern hangings,
banners, and candles. These should not be replaced until
the First Service of Easter. Crosses or images that are
veiled should remain so until the First Service of Easter.

29. GOOD FRIDAY

Year A (1981, 1984, 1987)

Isaiah 52:13–53:12; Hebrews 4:14-16; 5:7-9 or Hebrews
10:1-25; John 18:1–19:42
Psalm 22:1-18 or *Book of Hymns* 559
Hymns: 420, 430, 412

Year B (1979, 1982, 1985)

Isaiah 52:13–53:12; Hebrews 4:14-16; 5:7-9 or Hebrews
10:1-25; John 18:1–19:42
Psalm 31:1-5, 9-16 or *Book of Hymns* 559
Hymns: 415, 418, 420

Year C (1980, 1983, 1986)

Isaiah 52:13–53:12; Hebrews 4:14-16; 5:7-9 or Hebrews
10:1-25; John 18:1–19:42
Psalm 22:1-8, 19-31 or *Book of Hymns* 559
Hymns: 415, 418, 420

Opening Prayer

> Lord God,
> Jesus Christ was obedient unto death
>   that through his suffering on the cross
>   the disobedience of humanity
>   might give way to life.
> Give us new life through him
>   who died for our sins
>   and now lives and reigns
>   for ever and ever. **Amen.**

Or, opening prayer for Lent above.

Visuals

No colors, flowers, images, or decorative materials
should be used on Good Friday except, perhaps,
representations of the way of the cross. Altar tables,
pulpits, and lecterns should be bare of cloth, candles, or
anything else not actually used in the service. The Lord's
Supper should not be celebrated from Maundy Thursday
until the First Service of Easter.

EASTER SEASON

1. Opening Prayer for use in the Easter Season
   Lord of Life,
   by submitting to death
       you conquered the grave.
   By being lifted on a cross
       you draw all peoples to you.
   By being raised from the dead
       you restored to humanity
       all that we had lost through sin.
   Throughout these fifty days of Easter
       we proclaim the marvelous mystery
       of your death and resurrection.
   For all praise is yours
       now and throughout eternity. **Amen.**

2. Visuals
   The finest available—usually white, gold, yellow—
   and fine elegant textures. Bolts of brightly colored cloth
   may be slit half way lengthwise and hung across the
   nave, or brightness of color can be used in various ways
   to transform the building. The contrast to lenten array
   should be striking. Crosses ought to be avoided during
   the Easter Season except Christ reigning from the cross.
   Appropriate symbols for this season include the phoe-
   nix, butterflies, peacocks, pomegranate, or more abstract
   images such as a vertical arrow. Somberness of hue and
   rough textured material are put away for another day.
   If possible, the transformation from lenten to Easter
   visuals occurs at the lighting of a paschal candle. For this
   service and for the remainder of the Easter Season a large
   white candle (the paschal candle) at least two inches in
   diameter and two feet tall will be needed, plus a large
   candle stand at least three feet high. The paschal candle,
   like the morning star that never sets, signifies Christ
   shining eternally. It may be kept lighted at the front of the
   church for all services from Easter until the Day of
   Pentecost and then placed near the baptismal font for the
   remainder of the year.

30. EASTER EVE OR EASTER VIGIL OR THE FIRST SERVICE OF EASTER

Year A (1981, 1984, 1987)

Genesis 1:1–2:3; Psalm 33:1-11; Genesis 22:1-18; Psalm 33:12-22; Exodus 14:15–15:1; Exodus 15:1-6, 17-18; Isaiah 54:5-14; Psalm 30:2-6, 11-13; Isaiah 55:1-11; Isaiah 12:2-6; Ezekiel 36:16-28; Psalm 42:1-7; 43:3-4; Zephaniah 3:14-17, 19-20; Psalm 98; Romans 6:3-11; Psalm 114; Matthew 28:1-10

Hymns: 448/446 (Exodus/Matthew), 437 (Exodus/Matthew), 438, 480 (Genesis), 451, 452, 439, 443, 255 (for Psalm 42), 392 (for Psalm 98)

Year B (1979, 1982, 1985)

Same, except that the final lection is Mark 16:1-8

Year C (1980, 1983, 1986)

Same, except that the final lection is Luke 24:1-12

Opening prayer

God our deliverer,
This is the night (day) in which
  you saved your people from slavery.
This is the night (day) in which
  Christ broke the chains of death
  and rose triumphant from the grave.
This is the night (day) in which
  heaven is wedded to earth
  and humanity is reconciled to you.
May the light of your Word dispel all darkness
  and, like the morning star which never sets,
  shine without ceasing in our hearts.
For Christ your Son lives and reigns for ever. **Amen.**

> Adapted from the "Exsultet," *Sac.*

Or, opening prayer for Easter Day (Second Service of Easter) below.
Or, opening prayer for the Easter Season above.

Visuals

This is the ideal service at which to make the transformation from lenten to Easter visuals at the lighting of the paschal candle (see visuals for the Easter Season). In addition to the paschal candle, candles for the congregation and a large baptismal font filled with water are needed. If the cross or images are veiled during Lent, the veils can be removed during this service, especially at the lighting of the paschal candle.

31. EASTER DAY OR THE RESURRECTION OF THE LORD OR THE SECOND SERVICE OF EASTER

Year A (1981, 1984, 1987)

Acts 10:34-48* or Exodus 14:10-14, 21-25; 15:20-21; Colossians 3:1-11; John 20:1-18 or Matthew 28:1-10
Psalm 118:1-2, 14-24 or Book of Hymns 592
Hymns: 449, 454, 445, 448/446 (Exodus/Gospel)

Year B (1979, 1982, 1985)

Isaiah 25:6-9 or Acts 10:34-48*; I Corinthians 15:19-28 or Colossians 3:1-4; John 20:1-18 or Mark 16:1-8
Psalm 118:1-2, 14-24 or Book of Hymns 592
Hymns: 447, 445, 450

Year C (1980, 1983, 1986)

Exodus 15:1-11 or Acts 10:34-48*; I Corinthians 15:1-11 or Colossians 3:1-4; John 20:1-18 or Luke 24:1-35
Psalm 118:1-2, 14-24 or Book of Hymns 592
Hymns: 448/446 (Exodus/Gospel), 447, 437, "Every Morning Is Easter Morning"[11]
Opening prayer

> God our Father,
> by raising Christ your Son
>   you conquered the power of death
>   and opened to us the way to eternal life.
> Let our celebration today
>   raise us up and renew our lives
>   by the Spirit that is within us.
> Grant this through our Lord Jesus Christ, your Son,
>   who lives and reigns with you and the Holy Spirit,
>   one God, for ever and ever. **Amen.**   Sac.

Or, opening prayer for the Easter Season above.

Visuals
See Easter Season and Easter Eve (30).

---

*If the first lection is read from the Old Testament, the lection from Acts may be read as the second lection.

32. SECOND SUNDAY OF EASTER

Year A (1981, 1984, 1987)

Acts 2:14a, 22-32* or Genesis 8:6-16; 9:8-16; I Peter 1:3-9; John 20:19-31

Psalm 105:1-7 or Book of Hymns 605

Hymns: 450, 62, 419 (I Peter), "Jesus, the Lord of Life,"[12] BNC 5,[13] 133 (John), 137 (John), 48 (I Peter)

Year B (1979, 1982, 1985)

Acts 3:12a, 13-15, 17-26* or Isaiah 26:2-9, 19; I John 5:1-6; John 20:19-31

Psalm 148 or Book of Hymns 605

Hymns: 450, 115 (I John), "Jesus, the Lord of Life,"[12] 456

Year C (1980, 1983, 1986)

Acts 5:12-42* or Job 42:1-6; Revelation 1:4-19; John 20:19-31

Psalm 149 or Book of Hymns 605

Hymns: 445, 451, 440, 87, 455, 409 (Revelation)

33. THIRD SUNDAY OF EASTER

Year A (1981, 1984, 1987)

Acts 2:14a, 36-47* or Isaiah 43:1-12; I Peter 1:17-23; Luke 24:13-35

Psalm 16 or Book of Hymns 600

Hymns: 83, 421 (vv. 1, 3), 432, 289 (vv. 1, 3, 4—Luke), 313 (Luke) 281 (I Peter), 48 (Isaiah)

Year B (1979, 1982, 1985)

Acts 4:5-12* or Micah 4:1-5; I John 1:1–2:6; Luke 24:35-49

Psalm 139:1-12 or Book of Hymns 600

Hymns: 115, 278, 75, 410, 401, 89, 408 (Micah/I John)

Year C (1980, 1983, 1986)

Acts 9:1-20* or Jeremiah 32:36-41; Revelation 5:6-14; John 21:1-19

Psalm 30 or Book of Hymns 600

Hymns: 201, 341, 444, 274 (Acts), 107, 76 (Revelation)

---

*If the first lection is read from the Old Testament, the lection from Acts may be read as the second lection.

34. FOURTH SUNDAY OF EASTER
Year A (1981, 1984, 1987)

Acts 6:1-9; 7:2a, 51-60* or Nehemiah 9:6-15; I Peter 2:19-25; John 10:1-10

Psalm 23 or Book of Hymns 560

Hymns: 67 (John), 62, 340, 178, 80, WB 638 (Acts), WB 426[14]

Year B (1979, 1982, 1985)

Acts 4:23-37* or Ezekiel 34:1-10; I John 3:1-8; John 10:11-18

Psalm: 23 or Book of Hymns 560

Hymns: 201, 83, 67 (John), 278 (I John), 341 (Acts)

Year C (1980, 1983, 1986)

Acts 13:14-16, 26-39, 43* or Numbers 27:12-23; Revelation 7:9-17; John 10:22-30

Psalm 100 or Book of Hymns 560

Hymns: 129 (Revelation/John), 409, 453, 121, 83

35. FIFTH SUNDAY OF EASTER
Year A (1981, 1984, 1987)

Acts 17:1-15* or Deuteronomy 6:20-25; I Peter 2:1-10; John 14:1-14

Psalm 33:1-11 or Book of Hymns 565

Hymns: 75, 445 (John), 457, 81, WP 51 (I Peter), 298 (I Peter)

Year B (1979, 1982, 1985)

Acts 8:26-40* or Acts 9:26-31* or Deuteronomy 4:32-40; I John 3:18-24; John 15:1-8

Psalm 22:25-31 or Book of Hymns 565

Hymns: 530, 306, 287, 292, WB 619[15]

Year C (1980, 1983, 1986)

Acts 13:44-52* or Leviticus 19:1-2, 9-18; Revelation 21:1-5; John 13:31-35

Psalm 145:1-13 or Book of Hymns 565

Hymns: 456, 195 (Leviticus/John), 199 (Leviticus/John), 481 (Revelation), 62, 283, 409 (Acts)

*If the first lection is read from the Old Testament, the lection from Acts may be read as the second lection.

36. SIXTH SUNDAY OF EASTER

Year A (1981, 1984, 1987)

Acts 17:22-31* or Acts 8:4-8, 14-17* or Isaiah 41:17-20; I
Peter 3:8-22; John 14:15-21
Psalm 66:1-7, 16-20 or Books of Hymns 576
Hymns: 282, 309, 267, 283, 285, 341 (Acts/I Peter), SB 201[6]

Year B (1979, 1982, 1985)

Acts 11:19-30* or Isaiah 45:11-13, 18-19; I John 4:1-11;
John 15:9-17
Psalm 98 or Book of Hymns 576
Hymns: 62, 188, 173, 177, 149 (Acts), 41 (Isaiah)

Year C (1980, 1983, 1986)

Acts 14:8-28* or Acts 15:1-2, 22-29* or Joel 2:21-27;
Revelation 21:2-4, 10-14, 22-27; John 14:23-29
Psalm 64 or Book of Hymns 576
Hymns: 457, 481 (Revelation), 87, 267 (John)

*If the first lection is read from the Old Testament, the lection
from Acts may be read as the second lection.

37. ASCENSION DAY

(fortieth day—sixth Thursday—of Easter)
May be celebrated the Seventh Sunday of Easter.

Year A (1981, 1984, 1987)

Acts 1:1-11* or Daniel 7:9-14; Ephesians 1:15-23; Matthew
28:16-20 or Luke 24:44-53
Psalm 110 or Book of Hymns 561
Hymns: 454, 342 (Matthew), 409, 483

Year B (1979, 1982, 1985)

Acts 1:1-11* or Ezekiel 1:3-5a, 15-22, 26-28; Ephesians
1:15-23; Mark 16:9-20 or Luke 24:44-53
Psalm 110 or Book of Hymns 561
Hymns: 74, 71/72/73, 341, 292

Year C (1979, 1982, 1985)

Acts 1:1-11* or II Kings 2:1-15; Ephesians 1:15-23; Luke
24:44-53
Psalm 110 or Book of Hymns 561
Hymns: 76, 455, 410 (Luke)
Opening prayer

Loving God,
your only Son was taken up into heaven
 that he might prepare a place for us
 and send down the Spirit of Truth.
Make us joyful in his ascension
 so that we might worship him in his glory;
through Jesus Christ our Lord. **Amen.**

Sac. and CW6 altered

Visuals
 White. Abstract symbols such as a vertical arrow are
appropriate for this day and the Sunday following.

*If the first lection is read from the Old Testament, the lection
from Acts may be read as the second lection.

38. SEVENTH SUNDAY OF EASTER

Year A (1981, 1984, 1987)

Acts 1:1-14* or Ezekiel 39:21-29; I Peter 4:12-19; John 17:1-11

Psalm 47 or Book of Hymns 561

Hymns: 458 (Acts/I Peter), 530 (John), 306 (Acts/John), 233 (I Peter), 419 (I Peter), 409, 338, 228 (I Peter)

Year B (1979, 1982, 1985)

Acts 1:15-26* or Exodus 28:1-4, 9-10, 29-30; I John 4:11-21; John 17:11-19

Psalm 47 or Book of Hymns 561

Hymns: 456, 278, 476, 81, 125/126 (John), 261 (John), WB 641 (I John)

Year C (1980, 1983, 1986)

Acts 16:6-10, 16-34* or Acts 7:55-60* or I Samuel 12:19-24; Revelation 22:12-17, 20; John 17:20-26

Psalm 47 or Book of Hymns 561

Hymns: 193, 453, 243 (Acts), 456, 283

*If the first lection is read from the Old Testament, the lection from Acts may be read as the second lection.

39. THE DAY OF PENTECOST
OR THE DESCENT OF THE HOLY SPIRIT

Year A (1981, 1984, 1987)

Joel 2:28-32; Acts 2:1-21; John 20:19-23
Psalm 104:1-4, 24-33 or *Book of Hymns* 583
Hymns: 466, 467, *EUB* 148, 267, 133, 462, *MHSS* 66

Year B (1979, 1982, 1985)

Acts 2:1-21* or Ezekiel 37:1-14; I Corinthians 12:4-13; John 16:5-15
Psalm 104:1-4, 24-33 or *Book of Hymns* 583
Hymns: 136, 133, 135, 530 (I Corinthians), 297 (I Corinthians)

Year C (1980, 1983, 1986)

Genesis 11:1-9; Acts 2:1-21; John 15:26-27; 16:4b-11
Psalm 104:1-4, 24-33 or *Book of Hymns* 583
Hymns: 137 (John), 136 (Acts), 461, 132
Opening prayer

> Lord Jesus Christ,
> your church was born
>   in the power of the Holy Spirit.
> Send your Spirit into our lives
>   to break down all barriers of nation and race
>   and to unite all humanity in your praise;
> for you live and reign with the Father
>   and the Holy Spirit,
>   One God, for ever and ever. **Amen.**

Sac. altered

Visuals

Red, or the finest textures and brightest colors. The paschal candle should be moved before this service

*If the first lection is read from the Old Testament, the lection from Acts should be read as the second lection.

to a place near the baptismal font where it can remain until next year's Easter Eve (First Service of Easter). Appropriate Pentecost symbols include a descending dove, tongues of flame, symbols of the church (ship, rainbow) and, abstractly, a downward arrow. Since this is the birthday of the church, some people even get away with a birthday cake, especially when children are involved.

SEASON AFTER PENTECOST

1. Visuals

For this long season, red, green, or a combination of colors may be used. One very creative congregation used a variety of greens, changing from the yellowish greens of spring through bluer tones of summer and moving to reddish hues in autumn. Variety ought to be encouraged during this season; otherwise it becomes tedious and meaningless. The lections each Sunday may suggest ideas, especially if key images, words, or phrases are pinpointed.

40. FIRST SUNDAY AFTER PENTECOST OR TRINITY SUNDAY

Year A (1981, 1984, 1987)

Genesis 1:1–2:3; II Corinthians 13:5-14; Matthew 28:16-20
Psalm 150 or *Book of Hymns* 555
Hymns: 465, 277 (II Corinthians), 342 (Matthew), 459, 286, 462

Year B (1979, 1982, 1985)

Deuteronomy 4:32-34, 39-40; Romans 8:12-17; John 3:1-17
Psalm 149 or *Book of Hymns* 555
Hymns: 131, 133, 137 (John), 134, *CH* 357 (Deuteronomy/Romans), *MHSS* 47 (John)

Year C (1980, 1983, 1986)

Proverbs 8:22-31; Romans 5:1-5; John 16:12-15
Psalm 8 or *Book of Hymns* 555
Hymns: 466, 465 (Proverbs/Romans), 137, 259 (Romans)

Opening prayer

Father,
you sent your Word to bring us truth
 and your Spirit to make us holy.
Through them we come to know
 the mystery of your life.
Help us to worship you, one God in three persons,
 by proclaiming and living our faith in you.
Grant this through our Lord Jesus Christ, your Son,
 who lives and reigns with you and the Holy Spirit,
 one God, for ever and ever. **Amen.**   *Sac.*

Visuals

White. Appropriate symbols include the equilateral triangle, three intersecting circles, and other triune symbols, as long as all sides are equal.

91

41. SUNDAY BETWEEN MAY 29 AND JUNE 4 INCLUSIVE

(if after Trinity Sunday)

If the Sunday between May 24 and 28 inclusive follows Trinity Sunday, use 16 (Eighth Sunday after the Epiphany) on that day.

Year A (1981, 1984, 1987)

Deuteronomy 11:18-21, 26-28; Romans 3:21-28; Matthew 7:15-29

Psalm 31:1-5, 19-24 or *Book of Hymns* 606

Hymns: 129, 222 (Matthew), 281, 527, 139, 162, CH 307

Year B (1979, 1982, 1985)

Deuteronomy 5:12-15; II Corinthians 4:5-12; Mark 2:23–3:6

Psalm 81:1-10 or *Book of Hymns* 606

Hymns: 18, 460, 191, 106 (II Corinthians)

Year C (1980, 1983, 1986)

I Kings 8:22-23, 27-30, 41-43; Galatians 1:1-10; Luke 7:1-10

Psalm 117 or *Book of Hymns* 606

Hymns: 345 (I Kings/Galatians), 311, 293 (I Kings), 298, 192, "God of Truth, from Everlasting"[1]

42. SUNDAY BETWEEN JUNE 5 AND 11 INCLUSIVE
(if after Trinity Sunday)

Year A (1981, 1984, 1987)

Hosea 5:15–6:6; Romans 4:13-25; Matthew 9:9-13
Psalm 50:1-15 or *Book of Hymns* 570
Hymns: 111, 139, 104 (Matthew), 119, 208 (Romans), 221 (Romans), 102

Year B (1979, 1982, 1985)

Genesis 3:1-21; II Corinthians 4:13–5:1; Mark 3:20-35
Psalm 61:1-5, 8 or *Book of Hymns* 570
Hymns: 137, 114, 141 (II Corinthians), 145 (II Corinthians), 104, C 80

Year C (1980, 1983, 1986)

I Kings 17:17-24; Galatians 1:11-24; Luke 7:11-17
Psalm 30 or *Book of Hymns* 570
Hymns: 341, 109, 1, 277 (Galatians), 220 (Luke), 259 (Luke)

43. SUNDAY BETWEEN JUNE 12 AND 18 INCLUSIVE
(if after Trinity Sunday)

Year A (1981, 1984, 1987)

Exodus 19:2–8a; Romans 5:6-11; Matthew 9:35–10:15
Psalm 100 or *Book of Hymns* 611
Hymns: 527, 339 (Matthew), 122 (Romans), 58 (Exodus), 205 (Exodus/Romans), 195

Year B (1979, 1982, 1985)

Ezekiel 17:22-24; II Corinthians 5:1-10; Mark 4:26-34
Psalm 92 or *Book of Hymns* 611
Hymns: 462, 464 (Ezekiel/Mark), 471 (Ezekiel/Mark), 139 (II Corinthians), 142 (II Corinthians), 40 (Ezekiel)

Year C (1980, 1983, 1986)

II Samuel 11:26–12:10, 13-15; Galatians 2:11-21; Luke 7:36–8:3
Psalm 32 or *Book of Hymns* 611
Hymns: 279/280, 94, 114, 284, 124 (Galatians), 89, *MHSS* 9, CH 307

44. SUNDAY BETWEEN JUNE 19 AND 25 INCLUSIVE
(if after Trinity Sunday)

Year A (1981, 1984, 1987)

Jeremiah 20:7-13; Romans 5:12-21; Matthew 10:16-33
Psalm 69:1-18, 34-36 or *Book of Hymns* 574
Hymns: 244, 341, 241/240, 233, 212, 127 (Romans) "In the Presence of My Enemies"[16]

Year B (1979, 1982, 1985)

Job 38:1-11, 16-18; II Corinthians 5:14-21; Mark 4:35–5:20
Psalm 107:1-3, 23-32 or *Book of Hymns* 574
Hymns: "O Christ, My Lord, Create in Me,"[17] 209, 51 (Mark) 32 (Job), 36 (Job)

Year C (1980, 1983, 1986)

Zechariah 12:7-11; 13:1, Galatians 3:23-29; Luke 9:18-24
Psalm 63:1-8 or *Book of Hymns* 574
Hymns: 161, 297 (Zechariah/Luke), 153, 286, *BNC* 6, 170, *OHT* 62[18]

45. SUNDAY BETWEEN JUNE 26 AND JULY 2 INCLUSIVE

Year A (1981, 1984, 1987)

II Kings 4:8-16a; Romans 6:1-11; Matthew 10:34-42
Psalm 89:1-4, 15-18 or *Book of Hymns* 557
Hymns: *WB* 603[19], 204, 415, 184, 161, 115 (Romans), 160

Year B (1979, 1982, 1985)

Lamentations 3:22-33 or Wisdom 1:13-15; 2:23-24; II Corinthians 8:1-15; Mark 5:21-43
Psalm 30 or *Book of Hymns* 557
Hymns: 158/157, 177 (II Corinthians), 244, *SB* 201,[6] 499 (Lamentations), 53 (Lamentations), *CH* 561 (II Corinthians)

Year C (1980, 1983, 1986)

I Kings 19:14-21; Galatians 5:1, 13-25; Luke 9:51-62
Psalm 16 or *Book of Hymns* 557
Hymns: 150, 155, 161, "O Christ, My Lord, Create in Me,"[17] 281, *CH* 357

46. SUNDAY BETWEEN JULY 3 AND 9 INCLUSIVE

Year A (1981, 1984, 1987)

Zechariah 9:9-13; Romans 7:15–8:13; Matthew 11:25-30
Psalm 145 or Book of Hymns 602
Hymns: 117, 152, 125/126, 359, 119, 261, 483 (Zechariah)

Year B (1979, 1982, 1985)

Ezekiel 2:1-7; II Corinthians 12:7-10; Mark 6:1-6
Psalm 123 or Book of Hymns 602
Hymns: 460, 138, 150, 227, 220

Year C (1980, 1983, 1986)

Isaiah 66:10-16; Galatians 6:1-18; Luke 10:1-12, 16-20
Psalm 66:1-12, 16-20 or Book of Hymns 602
Hymns: 340, 124 (Galatians), 293 (Isaiah/Luke), 161, 311,
153, CH 555,[8] 261

47. SUNDAY BETWEEN JULY 10 AND 16 INCLUSIVE

Year A (1981, 1984, 1987)

Isaiah 55:1-5, 10-13; Romans 8:18-25; Matthew 13:1-23
Psalm 65 or Book of Hymns 575
Hymns: 464, UCC 200, 307, 460, 356, 371

Year B (1979, 1982, 1985)

Amos 7:7-17; Ephesians 1:1-14; Mark 6:7-13
Psalm 85:7-13 or Book of Hymns 575
Hymns: 341, 92 (Ephesians), 342 (Mark), 107

Year C (1980, 1983, 1986)

Deuteronomy 30:9-14; Colossians 1:1-20; Luke 10:25-37
Psalm 69:30, 32-36 or Book of Hymns 575
Hymns: 199, 156, 201, 161, 278 (Colossians), MHSS 38

48. SUNDAY BETWEEN JULY 17 AND 23 INCLUSIVE

Year A (1981, 1984, 1987)

Isaiah 44:6-8 or Wisdom 12:13, 16-19; Romans 8:26-27; Matthew 13:24-43
Psalm 86:11-17 or *Book of Hymns* 556
Hymns: 522 (vv. 2-4), 468, 137, 546, 475, EP 55

Year B (1979, 1982, 1985)

Jeremiah 23:1-6; Ephesians 2:11-22; Mark 6:30-44
Psalm 23 or *Book of Hymns* 556
Hymns: 83, 81, 102, 121 (Ephesians/Mark), 298 (Ephesians)

Year C (1980, 1983, 1986)

Genesis 18:1-14; Colossians 1:21-29; Luke 10:38-42
Psalm 15 or *Book of Hymns* 556
Hymns: "Sing Love Songs,"[20] 156, 341 (Colossians), 256

49. SUNDAY BETWEEN JULY 24 AND 30 INCLUSIVE

Year A (1981, 1984, 1987)

I Kings 3:5-12; Romans 8:28-30; Matthew 13:44-52
Psalm 119:129-36 or *Book of Hymns* 594
Hymns: 545 (vv. 1, 3, 5), *BNC* 6, 483, 484, 521 (Romans), 210 (Romans), 211 (Romans)

Year B (1979, 1982, 1985)

II Kings 4:42-44; Ephesians 4:1-7, 11-16; John 6:1-15
Psalm 145 or *Book of Hymns* 594
Hymns: 161, 369, 67, 301 (Ephesians), 109, 297 (Ephesians) 47 (II Kings)

Year C (1980, 1983, 1986)

Genesis 18:20-33; Colossians 2:6-15; Luke 11:1-13
Psalm 138 or *Book of Hymns* 594
Hymns: 487, 62 (Genesis/Colossians), 515 (Luke), 196, "Clap Your Hands"[21]

50. SUNDAY BETWEEN JULY 31
AND AUGUST 6 INCLUSIVE

Year A (1981, 1984, 1987)

Nehemiah 9:16-20; Romans 8:31-39; Matthew 14:13-21
Psalm 78:14-20, 23-29 or Book of Hymns 572
Hymns: 271, 307, 369, 221 (Romans), 521 (Romans), 329

Year B (1979, 1982, 1985)

Exodus 16:2-15; Ephesians 4:17-25; John 6:24-35
Psalm 78:14-20, 23-29 or Book of Hymns 572
Hymns: 329, 205, 369, 196 (Exodus/Ephesians), 271
(Exodus/John), 129, 103, 277 (Ephesians)

Year C (1980, 1983, 1986)

Ecclesiastes 1:2, 12-14; 2:1-7, 11, 18-26; Colossians 3:1-11;
Luke 12:13-21
Psalm 49:1-12 or Book of Hymns 572
Hymns: MHSS 11, 253 (Colossians), 286, 251, "All That I
Am,"[22] 182

51. SUNDAY BETWEEN AUGUST 7
AND 13 INCLUSIVE

Year A (1981, 1984, 1987)

I Kings 19:9-18; Romans 9:1-5; Matthew 14:22-33
Psalm 85:8-13 or Book of Hymns 566
Hymns: 235, 147, 247, 244, 209, 408 (Romans)

Year B (1979, 1982, 1985)

I Kings 19:4-8; Ephesians 4:25–5:2; John 6:37-51
Psalm 34:1-8 or Book of Hymns 566
Hymns: 369, 329, 102, 278 (Ephesians), 307, 207, 205

Year C (1980, 1983, 1986)

Genesis 15:1-6 or Wisdom 18:6-9; Hebrews 11:1-19; Luke
12:32-48
Psalm 33 or Book of Hymns 566
Hymns: WB 389, 181, 139 (Hebrews), 190, EP 74

52. SUNDAY BETWEEN AUGUST 14 AND 20 INCLUSIVE

Year A (1981, 1984, 1987)

Isaiah 56:1-8; Romans 11:13-16, 29-32; Matthew 15:21-28
Psalm 67 or Book of Hymns 567
Hymns: 292, EP 66, 408, 199, "God of Truth From Everlasting,"[1] 471

Year B (1979, 1982, 1985)

Proverbs 9:1-6, Ephesians 5:15-20; John 6:51-59
Psalm 34:9-14 or Book of Hymns 567
Hymns: 307, 102, 313 (John), WB 606[23] (Ephesians), CH 517,[24] EP 60 (John), 233 (Ephesians)

Year C (1980, 1983, 1986)

Jeremiah 38:1b-13; Hebrews 12:1-6; Luke 12:49-56
Psalm 82 or Book of Hymns 567
Hymns: 241/240, 249, 243, 242, 150

53. SUNDAY BETWEEN AUGUST 21 AND 27 INCLUSIVE

Year A (1981, 1984, 1987)

Isaiah 22:19-23; Romans 11:33-36; Matthew 16:13-20
Psalm 138 or Book of Hymns 578
Hymns: 409 (Romans/Matthew), 308 (Matthew), WP 51, 215 (Romans), 16

Year B (1979, 1982, 1985)

Joshua 24:1-2a, 14-25; Ephesians 5:21-33; John 6:60-69
Psalm 34:15-22 or Book of Hymns 578
Hymns: 101, 159, 470, 164, 18, 297 (Ephesians), UCC 175[25] (Ephesians)

Year C (1980, 1983, 1986)

Isaiah 66:18-23; Hebrews 12:7-13; Luke 13:22-30
Psalm 117 or Book of Hymns 578
Hymns: 468, OHT 62,[18] 242, 477, 105

54. SUNDAY BETWEEN AUGUST 28 and SEPTEMBER 3 INCLUSIVE

Year A (1981, 1984, 1987)

Jeremiah 15:15-21; Romans 12:1-8; Matthew 16:21-28
Psalm 26 or *Book of Hymns* 586
Hymns: 242, EP 113, 415, 251, C 124, "Many Gifts, One Spirit"[26]

Year B (1979, 1982, 1985)

Deuteronomy 4:1-8; Ephesians 6:10-20; Mark 7:1-8, 14-15, 21-23
Psalm 15 or *Book of Hymns* 586
Hymns: 250 (Ephesians), 156, 188, 282 (Mark), 279/280 (Mark)

Year C (1980, 1983, 1986)

Proverbs 25:6-7 or Ecclesiastes 3:17-18, 20, 28-29; Hebrews 12:18–13:8; Luke 14:1, 7-14
Psalm 112 or *Book of Hymns* 586
Hymns: 201, 178, 254, 177

55. SUNDAY BETWEEN SEPTEMBER 4 AND 10 INCLUSIVE

Year A (1981, 1984, 1987)

Ezekiel 33:1-11; Romans 12:9–13:10; Matthew 18:15-20
Psalm 119:33-40 or *Book of Hymns* 604
Hymns: 301, 193, 475 (Ezekiel), 309, UCC 183, 266

Year B (1979, 1982, 1985)

Isaiah 35:4-7a; James 1:17-27; Mark 7:31-37
Psalm 146 or *Book of Hymns* 604
Hymns: 201, 1 (Isaiah/Mark), 199 (James), 125/126, 212 CH 163

Year C (1980, 1983, 1986)

Proverbs 9:8-12 or Wisdom 9:13-18; Philemon 1-21; Luke 14:25-33
Psalm 10:12-14, 16-18 or *Book of Hymns* 604
Hymns: 251, SS 7[7], 259, OHT 62,[18] 152, 182, 167

56. SUNDAY BETWEEN SEPTEMBER 11
AND 17 INCLUSIVE

Year A (1981, 1984, 1987)

Genesis 50:15-21 or Ecclesiasticus 27:30–28:7; Romans 14:5-12; Matthew 18:21-35

Psalm 103:1-13 or *Book of Hymns* 588

Hymns: *MHSS 9, 469 (Genesis/Matthew), 218 (Romans), 282, 114, 52 (Genesis), 69*

Years B (1979, 1982, 1985)

Isaiah 50:4-10; James 2:1-5, 8-10, 14-18; Mark 8:27-38 or Mark 9:14-29

Psalm 116:1-9 or *Book of Hymns* 588

Hymns: 160 (Mark 8), 177 (James), 217 (Isaiah), 159 (Mark 8), 170, *SS* 7[7] (James)

Year C (1980, 1983, 1986)

Exodus 32:1, 7-14; I Timothy 1:12-17; Luke 15:1-32

Psalm 51:1-17 or *Book of Hymns* 588

Hymns: 479, 175, 196 (I Timothy/Luke), 195, *OHT* 49, 27 (I Timothy)

57. SUNDAY BETWEEN SEPTEMBER 18
AND 24 INCLUSIVE

Year A (1981, 1984, 1987)

Isaiah 55:6-11; Philippians 1:1-11, 19-27; Matthew 20:1-16

Psalm 27:1-9 or *Book of Hymns* 601

Hymns: 206, *BNC* 6, 159 (Philippians), 203, 65 (Isaiah) 190, *BNC* 8, *EP* 113

Year B (1979, 1982, 1985)

Jeremiah 11:18-20 or Wisdom 1:16–2:1, 6-22; James 3:13–4:6; Mark 9:30-37

Psalm 54 or *Book of Hymns* 601

Hymns: 80, 178, 184, 161, 211 (Jeremiah), 244 (Jeremiah), 286

Year C (1980, 1983, 1986)

Amos 8:4-12; I Timothy 2:1-8; Luke 16:1-13

Psalm 113 or *Book of Hymns* 601

Hymns: 254, 156, 470, *SS* 7,[7] 484 (Amos), 242

58. SUNDAY BETWEEN SEPTEMBER 25 AND OCTOBER 1 INCLUSIVE

Year A (1981, 1984, 1987)

Ezekiel 18:1-4, 25-32; Philippians 2:1-13; Matthew 21: 28-32

Psalm 25:1-10 or *Book of Hymns* 603

Hymns: 119, 356, 477, 528, 242, 475 (Ezekiel), 74 (Philippians)

Year B (1979, 1982, 1985)

Numbers 11:4-6, 10-16, 24-30; James 4:7–5:6; Mark 9:38-50

Psalm 135:1-7, 13-14 or *Book of Hymns* 603

Hymns: 479, 87, *BNC* 4, 188, 199, 286, SS 7[7] (James)

Year C (1980, 1983, 1986)

Amos 6:1-7; I Timothy 6:6-19; Luke 16:19-31

Psalm 146 or *Book of Hymns* 603

Hymns 164, 188, 256, 484, 231 (I Timothy), 282, SS 7,[7] *BNC* 6

59. SUNDAY BETWEEN OCTOBER 2 AND 8 INCLUSIVE

Year A (1981, 1984, 1987)

Isaiah 5:1-7; Philippians 3:12-21; Matthew 21:33-43

Psalm 80:7-15, 18-19 or *Book of Hymns* 607

Hymns: 546, 356, *UCC* 182, *WB* 389, 355, 204, 483 (Philippians)

Year B (1979, 1982, 1985)

Genesis 2:18-24; Hebrews 2:1-18; Mark 10:2-16

Psalm 128 or *Book of Hymns* 607

Hymns: 162, 121, 178, 124 (Hebrews), 85 Hebrews), *UCC* 175 [25] (Genesis/Mark)

Year C (1980, 1983, 1986)

Habakkuk 1:1-13; 2:1-4; II Timothy 1:1-14; Luke 17:1-10

Psalm 95:1-7 or *Book of Hymns* 607

Hymns: 142, 141, 152, 341 (II Timothy), 149 (II Timothy), 210, 462

60. SUNDAY BETWEEN OCTOBER 9 AND 15 INCLUSIVE

Year A (1981, 1984, 1987)

Isaiah 25:1-10*a*; Philippians 4:4-20; Matthew 22:1-14
Psalm 23 or *Book of Hymns* 579
Hymns: 207 (Isaiah/Philippians), "The Wedding Banquet,"[27] (Matthew), 460 (Isaiah), 544 (Isaiah), 325 (Matthew), 218 (Philippians), 102 (Matthew)

Year B (1979, 1982, 1985)

Amos 5:6-7, 10-15 or Wisdom 7:7-11; Hebrews 3:1-6; Mark 10:17-31
Psalm 90:1-8, 12-17 or *Book of Hymns* 579
Hymns: 187, 107, 75, 173, HFL 491[2]

Year C (1980, 1983, 1986)

Ruth 1:1-19*a*; II Timothy 2:3-15; Luke 17:11-19
Psalm 111 or *Book of Hymns* 579
Hymns: 196, *BNC* 4, 243 (II Timothy), 160 (II Timothy), 141

61. SUNDAY BETWEEN OCTOBER 16 AND 22 INCLUSIVE

Year A (1981, 1984, 1987)

Isaiah 45:1-7; I Thessalonians 1:1-5*a*; Matthew 22:15-22
Psalm 96 or *Book of Hymns* 595
Hymns: 153, 548, 181, 8 (Isaiah), 14 (Isaiah), 470

Year B (1979, 1982, 1985)

Isaiah 53:4-12; Hebrews 4:9-16; Mark 10:35-45
Psalm 91:9-16 or *Book of Hymns* 595
Hymns: 161, 80, 203, 413, 420, CH 552[4]

Year C (1980, 1983, 1986)

Genesis 32:3-8, 22-30 or Exodus 17:8-13; II Timothy 3:14–4:5; Luke 18:1-8
Psalm 121 or *Book of Hymns* 595
Hymns: 207, 140, 529 (Genesis), 371 (II Timothy), 231 (Luke), 460 (II Timothy), 356 (II Timothy)

62. SUNDAY BETWEEN OCTOBER 23
AND 29 INCLUSIVE

Year A (1981, 1984, 1987)

Exodus 22:21-27; I Thessalonians 1:5b–2:8; Matthew 22:34-46

Psalm 18:1-3, 46, 50 or *Book of Hymns* 596

Hymns: 199, 242, 281, 182 (Matthew), 188, 475, 469 (Exodus)

Year B (1979, 1982, 1985)

Jeremiah 31:7-9, Hebrews 5:1-10; Mark 10:46-52

Psalm 126 or *Book of Hymns* 596

Hymns: 235, 158/157, 81, 154, CH 163, 1

Year C (1980, 1983, 1986)

Deuteronomy 10:12-22 or Ecclesiasticus 35:12-18; II Timothy 4:6-8, 16-18; Luke 18:9-14

Psalm 34:1-2, 15-22 or *Book of Hymns* 596

Hymns: 211, 256, 56, 241/240, 172 (Luke), 138 (Luke)

63. SUNDAY BETWEEN OCTOBER 30
AND NOVEMBER 5 INCLUSIVE

Year A (1981, 1984, 1987)

Malachi 1:14b–2:10; I Thessalonians 2:7-13, 17-20; Matthew 23:1-12
Psalm 131 or *Book of Hymns* 593
Hymns: 309, 254, 369 (I Thessalonians), 109 (I Thessalonians), 188, 65 (Malachi)

Year B (1979, 1982, 1985)

Deuteronomy 6:1-9; Hebrews 7:23-28; Mark 12:28-34
Psalm 119:1-16 or *Book of Hymns* 593
Hymns: 202, 188, 194, 65 (Deuteronomy), 182

Year C (1980, 1983, 1986)

Exodus 34:5-9 or Wisdom 11:23–12:2; II Thessalonians 1:1–2:2; Luke 19:1-10
Psalm 145 or *Book of Hymns* 593
Hymns: 475 (Exodus/II Thessalonians), 469 (Exodus/II Thessalonians), 159 (II Thessalonians/Luke), 175 (Luke), 201 (Luke), 470, *BNC* 16

64. SUNDAY BETWEEN NOVEMBER 6 AND 12 INCLUSIVE

Year A (1981, 1984, 1987)

Amos 5:18-24 or Wisdom 6:12-16; I Thessalonians 4:13-18; Matthew 25:1-13

Psalm 63:1-7 or Book of Hymns 589

Hymns: EUB 75, 474 (I Thessalonians), 366, 363, 302 (I Thessalonians), 102, EUB 138

Year B (1979, 1982, 1985)

I Kings 17:8-16; Hebrews 9:24-28; Mark 12:38-44

Psalm 146 or Book of Hymns 589

Hymns: 521, 523, 176, 353 (Hebrews)

Year C (1980, 1983, 1986)

Job 19:23-27a or II Maccabees 7:1-2, 9-14; II Thessalonians 2:13–3:5; Luke 20:27-38

Psalm 17 or Book of Hymns 589

Hymns: 440, 445 (Job/Luke), 371, 471, 477, 464, WP 51

65. SUNDAY BETWEEN NOVEMBER 13 AND 19 INCLUSIVE

Year A (1981, 1984, 1987)

Proverbs 31:10-13, 19-20, 30-31 or Zephaniah 1:7, 12-18; I Thessalonians 5:1-11; Matthew 25:14-30

Psalm 128 or Book of Hymns 613

Hymns: 177, 150, (I Thessalonians), 181, 364 (I Thessalonians) 477

Year B (1979, 1982, 1985)

Daniel 12:1-13; Hebrews 10:11-18, 31-39; Mark 13:14-32

Psalm 16 or Book of Hymns 613

Hymns: 222, 474, 464, BNC 4, 17, 228

Year C (1980, 1983, 1986)

Malachi 3:13–4:2a, 5-6; II Thessalonians 3:6-13; Luke 21:5-19

Psalm 98 or Book of Hymns 613

Hymns: 48, 152 (II Thessalonians), 150 (II Thessalonians), 222, UCC 64

66. LAST SUNDAY AFTER PENTECOST
OR CHRIST THE KING
(Sunday between November 20 and 26 inclusive)

Year A (1981, 1984, 1987)

Ezekiel 34:11-17, 23-24; I Corinthians 15:20-28; Matthew 25:31-46
Psalm 95:1-7 or *Book of Hymns* 582
Hymns: 201, 362, 458 (I Corinthians), 483, 546

Year B (1979, 1982, 1985)

Daniel 7:13-14; Revelation 1:1-8; John 18:33-37
Psalm 93 or *Book of Hymns* 582
Hymns: 477, 357 (Revelation), 545, 372, 76, 220

Year C (1980, 1983, 1986)

II Samuel 5:1-4 or Jeremiah 23:1-6; Colossians 1:11-20; Luke 23:35-43
Psalm 46 or *Book of Hymns* 582
Hymns: 76, 298, 471, 454, 78
Opening prayer

> All-powerful God,
> your only Son came to earth
>   in the form of a slave
>   and is now enthroned at your right hand,
>   where he rules in glory.
> As he reigns as King in our hearts,
>   may we rejoice in his peace,
>   glory in his justice,
>   and live in his love.
> For with you and the Holy Spirit
>   he rules now and for ever.
> **Amen.**   *Sac.* altered

Visuals

White. Symbols of royalty may be used—crown, orb, scepter—especially when these contain, or are combined with, a cross. Images of Christ as Pantocrator (ruler of all) seated on a throne and blessing the world are appropriate.

67. ALL SAINTS' DAY

(November 1)

May be celebrated the first Sunday in November.

Year A (1981, 1984, 1987)

Isaiah 26:1-4, 8-9, 12-13, 19-21 or Ecclesiasticus 44:1-10, 13-14

Revelation 21:9-11, 22-27; 22:1-5; Matthew 5:1-12

Psalm 24:1-6 or *Book of Hymns* 566

Hymns: 304, 303, 288, 56 (Isaiah), 276 (Matthew)

Year B (1979, 1982, 1985)

Revelation 7:2-4, 9-17* or Ecclesiasticus 44:1-10, 13-14; I John 3:1-3; Matthew 5:1-12

Psalm 24:1-6 or *Book of Hymns* 566

Hymns: 536/537, 304, 291, 276 (Matthew)

Year C (1980, 1983, 1986)

Isaiah 26:1-4, 8-9, 12-13, 19-21 or Ecclesiasticus 2:1-11; Ephesians 1:11-23; Luke 6:20-36

Psalm 149 or *Book of Hymns* 566

Hymns: 151, 76 (Ephesians), 245 (Isaiah), 115, 483 (Ephesians)

Opening prayer

God of all holiness,
you gave your saints different gifts on earth
but one holy city in heaven.
Give us the grace to follow their good examples,
that we may know the joy you have prepared

for all who love you;
through your Son, Jesus Christ our Lord.
Amen.   *Sac.* and *CW6* altered

Visuals

White, signifying that it is Christ who lives in the saints. Visual symbols can include myriads of paper dolls (each marked by a cross), a cloud of witnesses, silhouettes representing all races and both sexes, a

*May be read as the second lection.

107

calendar of saints, an assemblage of vertical arrows of different colors, different types of the numeral or word *one*, symbols of the church used on the Day of Pentecost.

If a procession is held, each person may be asked to carry a placard with the name of the saint who means the most to him or her (be prepared for some strange names). As people enter, these may be made on posterboard, or all entering may write names on a large poster. Someone may read from a calendar of saints—listing names, century, and occupation—such as: Lydia, first century, merchant; Thomas Aquinas, thirteenth century, theologian; John Bunyan, seventeenth century, tinker; Florence Nightingale, nineteenth century, nurse; and so on.

Names of those in the congregation who have died within the past year should be read and perhaps printed in the bulletin.

JOHN WESLEY AND ALL SAINTS' DAY: EXCERPTS FROM HIS JOURNAL

Compiled by Professor Laurence H. Stookey

1748—Tuesday, Nov. 1. Being All Saints' Day, we had a solemn assembly at the chapel, as I cannot but observe we have had on this very day for several years. Surely, "right dear in the sight of the Lord is the death of his saints."

1756—Monday, Nov. 1 was a day of triumphant joy, as All Saints' Day generally is. How superstitious are they who scruple giving God solemn thanks for the lives and deaths of his saints!

1766—Saturday, Nov. 1. "God, who hath knit together his elect in one communion and fellowship" gave us a solemn season at West Street, as usual, in praising him for all his saints. On this day in particular, I commonly find the truth of these words (by Charles Wesley):

The Church triumphant in his love,

Their mighty joys we know;

They praise the Lamb in hymns above,

And we in hymns below.

1767—Sunday, Nov. 1. Being All Saints' Day (a festival I dearly love,) I could not but observe the admirable propriety with which the Collect, the Epistle, and Gospel for the day are suited to each other.

1778—Sunday, Nov. 1 was the day appointed for opening the new chapel in the City Road . . . . In the afternoon when I preached on the hundred and forty-four thousand standing with the Lamb on Mount Zion, God was eminently present in the midst of the congregation.

1788—Saturday, Nov. 1. Being All Saints' Day, I preached at Snowfields on Rev. 14:1—a comfortable subject; and I always find this a comfortable day.

1789—Sunday, Nov. 1. Being All Saints' Day, a day that I peculiarly love, I preached on Rev. 7:1; and we rejoiced with solemn joy.

NOTES

1. By Florence E. Cain, in *Music Ministry*, January 1972; also from Hymn Society of America, Wittenberg University, Springfield, Ohio 45501.
2. "Make Us, O God, a Church That Shares," also in *Music Ministry*, January 1974.
3. By Elbert N. Johnson, in *Ten New Hymns on the Ministry*, Hymn Society of America.
4. "The City Is Alive, O God;" also at HFL 504 with less appropriate tune. Words and suggestions for tunes given in *Music Ministry*, January 1973. Words from Hymn Society of America.
5. By Carlton C. Buck, in *Music Ministry*, June 1972; also from Hymn Society of America.
6. "Our Hope Is in the Living God," by Ernest K. Emurian. Tune: ST. CATHERINE. Also in *Seven New Hymns of Hope*, Hymn Society of America.
7. "See How Swarming Birds of Heaven;" also in *Music Ministry*, June 1977.
8. "O Lord, the Maze of Earthly Ways," by Carlton C. Buck; also from Hymn Society of America. Try tune AMAZING GRACE.
9. "The Earth Is the Lord's" ("God in His Love for Us"), by F. Pratt Green, in *Music Ministry*, October 1975; also from Hymn Society of America.
10. "Jesus Walked This Lonesome Valley;" also in many recent folk-style song collections.
11. By Richard Avery and Donald March, in The Avery and Marsh Songbook (Proclamation Productions, Port Jervis, New York 12771); also available on single sheets.
12. In *The Hymn*, July 1973, from the Hymn Society of America. Tune: DIADEMATA.
13. "Each Sunday Brings to Mind Again;" also in *Music Ministry*, January 1977.
14. "Lord of the Dance" ("I Danced in the Morning"), found also in many recent folk- and pop-style songbooks.
15. "We Are One in the Spirit" ("They'll Know We Are Christians by Our Love"), found in many recent hymnals and other song collections.
16. "In the Presence of My Enemies," by Richard Avery and Donald Marsh, in *Number 7*, available from Proclamation Productions.
17. "O Christ, My Lord, Create in Me," by Chester E. Custer, in *Music Ministry*, June 1974. Tune: RETREAT.
18. "Lord of All Power, I Give You My Will," by Jack C. Winslow; also in *Music Ministry*, July 1978. Tune: SLANE.
19. "Thou, Whose Purpose Is to Kindle." Alternate tune: HYFRYDOL.
20. By Richard Avery and Donald Marsh, in *The Avery and Marsh Songbook;* also available on single sheets.
21. By Ray Repp, in a number of current folk- and pop-style song collections.
22. By Sebastian Temple, in *Songbook for Saints and Sinners* (Hope Publishing Company, Carol Stream, Illinois 60187).
23. "Simple Gifts" (the Shaker song), found also in a number of folk- and pop-style song collections.

24. "Sons of God," by James Thiem, found also in recent pop-style song collections.
25. May be sung to the tune PERFECT LOVE.
26. By Al Carmines, in *Go to Galilee*, available from Chappell and Company, 810 Seventh Avenue, New York, New York 10019
27. "The Wedding Banquet," in *Joy Is Like the Rain*, by Sister Miriam Therese Winter (Vanguard Music Corporation, 250 West 57th Street, New York, New York 10019.)

—IV—
RESOURCES FOR SPECIAL OCCASIONS

1. At Baptism, Confirmation, and Renewal

God of Love,
in baptism we are united to Christ
  and grafted as living members to his body, your church.
We ask that all who are made Christians this day
  may be strengthened by your Spirit.
  May they never be ashamed to confess
  that Jesus is Lord.
We ask this in the name of Jesus the Christ. **Amen.**

2. At Services of Reconciliation

God, our Father and Mother,
you created us to live in harmony
  with each other and all creation.
Forgive our discords, and make us a people of love,
  so that we may be reconciled to you and to each other.
We ask this in the name of Jesus our Lord. **Amen.**

3. At Ordinations

Lord God,
in all generations you have chosen women and men
  to make your will known on earth.
Breathe your Holy Spirit
  on those whom we ordain to your service today
  that their whole lives may be signs of your love.
We ask this through our Lord Jesus Christ. **Amen.**

4. At Weddings

God our Creator,
when you created humanity
  you willed that husband and wife
  should be one flesh.
Bind (name) and (name)
  in the loving union of marriage,
  that their bond may be a living witness
  to your divine love as long as they live.
We ask this through Christ our Lord. **Amen.**

5. At Services of Healing

All-powerful God, Source of all life and health,
accept our prayers
  for our sisters and brothers who are ill,
and in your wisdom
  sustain them as is best.
Grant this through Christ our Lord. **Amen.**

6. At Funerals

God of steadfast love,
your love never ends.
When all else has failed,
  you still remain our God.
You gave your only Son up to death
  that we might share in his death and resurrection.
Now in this moment of sorrow,
  give us the faith and hope
  to entrust our loved one to your keeping
  with sure confidence in your unending love;
through Jesus Christ our Lord. **Amen.**

7. At Thanksgiving Services

Lord our God,
love began with you
  and has filled our cup to overflowing.
In the abundance of your countless gifts,
  give us your grace

to fill others' lives with love,
that we may more nearly be worthy
of all you have given us.
We ask this in the name of Jesus the Lord. **Amen.**

8. At Civic Occasions

Righteous God,
you have made us one nation,
   gathered from all the peoples of the earth.
Confirm in us a love of liberty and justice for all.
You have given us so much;
   help us to remember that you expect much of us.
We ask this through Jesus Christ our Lord,
   who lives and reigns with you and the Holy Spirit,
   one God, for ever and ever. **Amen.**

9. At Services for Social Justice

Lord of mercy and justice,
you entered this world powerless as a baby
   and died helpless on a cross.
Help us experience the sufferings
   of those who are powerless and oppressed,
   so that our indifference or abuse
   will not increase their suffering.
We ask this in your name, Lord Christ. **Amen.**

10. At Wesleyan Occasions

God of all history,
through the sermons and hymns
   of John and Charles Wesley
   you called to the light of truth
   those who walked in darkness.
Keep us true to the faith
   the Wesleys professed with untiring zeal,
   and help us grow to perfection in lives of love.
We ask this through Christ our Lord. **Amen.**

—V—
INDEXES

Scripture Lections

115

New Testament

Matthew

Mark

Luke

John

Romans

Apocrypha

Wisdom (of Solomon)

Ecclesiasticus (Sirach)

Baruch

II Maccabees

The Psalter

Hymns

( )indicates the number in *The Book of Hymns* (*The Methodist Hymnal*) or the source if not in *The Book of Hymns*.

First Lines   **Day/Year**

A charge to keep I have (150)..............45C, 46B, 52C, 65A, 65C
Abide with me; fast falls the eventide (289)........................ 33A

SEASONS OF THE GOSPEL